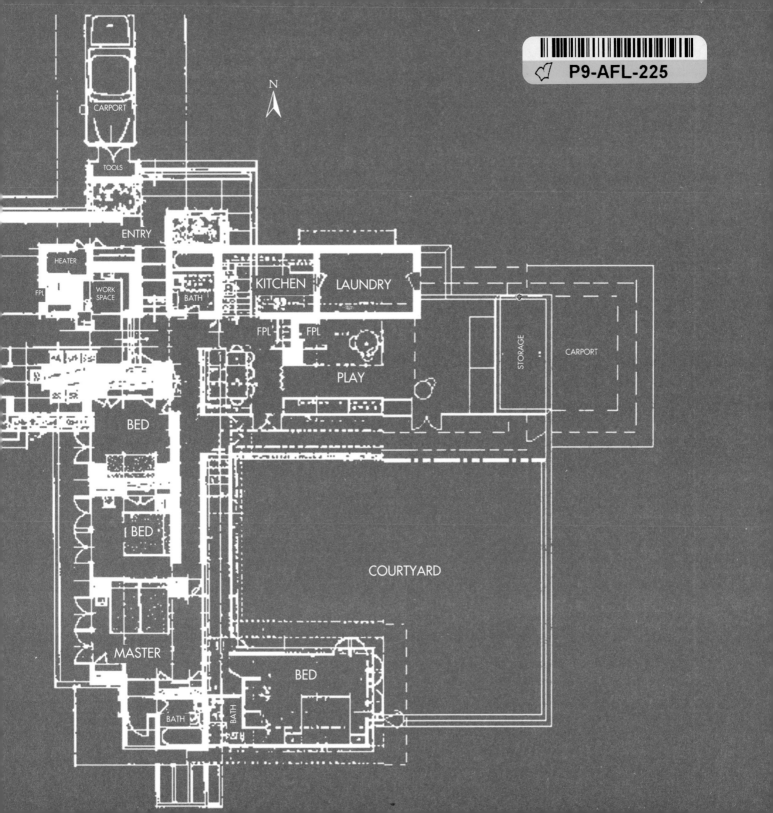

USONIA

ALVIN ROSENBAUM

FOREWORD BY FREDERICK GUTHEIM

USONIA

FRANK LLOYD WRIGHT'S DESIGN FOR AMERICA

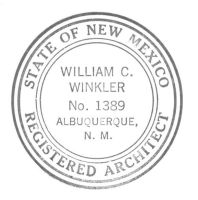
THE PRESERVATION PRESS
NATIONAL TRUST FOR HISTORIC PRESERVATION

The Preservation Press
National Trust for Historic Preservation
1785 Massachusetts Avenue, N.W.
Washington D.C. 20036

The National Trust for Historic Preservation is the only private, nonprofit organization chartered by Congress to encourage public participation in the preservation of sites, buildings, and objects significant in American history and culture. In carrying out this mission, the National Trust fosters an appreciation of the diverse character and meaning of our American cultural heritage and preserves and revitalizes the livability of our communities by leading the nation in saving America's historic environments.

Support for the National Trust is provided by membership dues, contributions, and a matching grant from the National Park Service, the U.S. Department of the Interior, under provisions of the National Historic Preservation Act of 1966. The opinions expressed here do not necessarily reflect the views or policies of the Interior Department.

Printed in Singapore
97 96 95 94 93   5 4 3 2 1

Library of Congress Cataloging in Publication Data

Rosenbaum, Alvin
      Usonia: Frank Lloyd Wright's design for America / Alvin Rosenbaum.
            p.   cm.
      ISBN 0-89133-201-4
      1. Usonian houses—United States. 2. Wright, Frank Lloyd, 1867-1959—Criticism and
      interpretation. I. Title.
NA7208.R67 1993
728' .37' 092—dc20   93-7612

CONTENTS

(Opposite) A Broadacre City vista from Frank Lloyd Wright's 1958 *The Living City*

ACKNOWLEDGMENTS

The community of architects and homeowners, scholars, archivists, and students of the life and work of Frank Lloyd Wright have been extraordinarily friendly and unselfishly helpful in assisting my work. I am particularly grateful to my friends at Taliesin, who provided a perfectly complete and beautiful setting for me to begin my research. I wish particularly to thank Bruce Brooks Pfeiffer of the Frank Lloyd Wright Archives and members of his staff, Indira Berndtson, Oscar R. Munoz, and Margo Stipe, whose enthusiasm for their work made mine that much more pleasurable.

Over the past two years I have made many new friends, at Taliesin, through the Frank Lloyd Wright Building Conservancy, and through the dozens of contacts made on my travels and by telephone. I was delighted by my initial encounter with Frederick Gutheim, Frank Lloyd Wright's first archivist. Fritz Gutheim became my teacher and friend, a man with total recall of events spanning more than half a century and providing insights and continuous direction that were both tireless and inspired. I also wish to thank Edgar Tafel, whose wit was a constant reminder to me of Frank Lloyd Wright's own sense of humor.

I am grateful to John Sergeant, who guided me and whose book, *Frank Lloyd Wright's Usonian Houses*, is a landmark, and to my older brother, Jonathan, whose own family memoir, *Meeting Places, A Life at the Movies*, published in 1980, was an inspiration to my work.

I also wish to thank Dean Steven W. Hurtt amd his colleagues John W. Hill and David Fogle at the University of Maryland School of Architecture who afforded me extraordinary access to university resources..

Many others along this fascinating path have been gracious in their hospitality and helpful to my work, including Margaret Klinkow, Carla Lind, John Meunier, Patricia Bunnell, Mary and William Palmer, Marshall Erdman, Joanne Chung, Mary Tolbert Matheny, James Tolbert, Robert Whitten, Nancy Gonce, Loren Pope, Darwin Matthew, Anthony Wren, Sally Sims Stokes, Katherine Jacobs, Susan Jacobs Lockhart, Abigail Malamed, Mary Miller, Chalmers Hood, Richard Guy Wilson, John O. Holzhueter, and George O. Talbot.

I am indebted to the publishing team at the National Trust for Historic Preservation, including Buckley Jeppson, Janet Walker, Margaret Gore Johnson, and my editor, Cynthia Ware. Most of all, I am grateful to my mother, Mildred Rosenbaum. I dedicate this book to her and to the memory of my father, Stanley Rosenbaum.

Chevy Chase, Maryland

May 1993

FOREWORD BY FREDERICK GUTHEIM

In the 1991 Guggenheim Foundation awards I noticed one for the writing of an opera based on the life of Frank Lloyd Wright. At last, I thought, the enigma that has defeated Wright biographers, architecture critics, historians, and others simply interested in the great architect might be finally laid open. All this was before I had read Alvin Rosenbaum's exploration of Wright's quest for his ideal dwelling, the Usonian house. Further, Rosenbaum joins this search to his still larger view of the ideal community—what Wright called Broadacre City, a utopian fantasy that lived only in architectural models and drawings, incorporating a variety of ideal buildings, many of which can be traced to Wright's early career. Of all the attempts to explain the forms that Wright's genius took, this book is the most satisfactory. By joining Broadacre City with the Usonian house, Rosenbaum has arrived at a unified account of Wright's creative effort.

For those who have searched out Wright-designed buildings to fathom the depths of their mysterious charm, for readers of Wright's *Autobiography* and those who have studied his endless pronouncements of how we should live, and for those who found in his lifestyle itself the ultimate answer to modern life's dissatisfactions, the solution is finally clear: in this record, one answer, whether in the form of buildings, writings, or life itself, explains the other.

Rosenbaum grew up living in a Wright house. He witnessed the seminal regional planning exercise of the early Tennessee Valley Authority. He shared briefly but critically important experience as a member of the Taliesin Fellowship. There is no substitute for such experience. It allows him to connect with the larger dimensions of Wright's creative activity. His presentation is the first all-dimensional perspective on the architect's buildings, writings, and life, a prism in which we can relate what is told here to other elements in Wright's oeuvre, a master key to the greatest cornucopia of the larger world of architecture.

The origin of the Usonian house has been traced to those turn-of-the century cottages that Wright designed for the pages of *Ladies' Home Journal* at the turn of the century. In their mature form they reflected the housing shortages that flourished in the Great Depression and the great wars when building stopped but people kept having babies. But unlike other dreamers and purveyors of "model houses" Wright broke the barriers of building codes and housing finance. The Usonian houses escaped to the far suburbs beyond the code jurisdictions. For building money he flirted with Major Douglas, social credit, and *Freiwirtschaft*.

The Usonian houses were truly innovative. Wright claimed with justification that he killed the dining room (by moving the function to the end of the living room). Further economies he derived from built-in furniture and storage and by extending living areas to the out-of-doors. Many of these strategies can be seen in the Millard house in California, the Robie house, or the Jacobs house. The Pope-Leighey House, now a property of the National Trust for Historic Preservation and thus accessible to visitors, illustrates many of these points. Wright was alert to the social and economic changes that were altering the household economy, outstanding among which was the disappearance of servants and the rationalization of household work.

Broadacre City was a unique creation in the form of a large model. There are comparable exercises, such as Richard Neutra's Rush City, which is not nearly as comprehensive, and really more exclusively represents a southern Californian reflection of an automobile-dominated society. Le Corbusier's Radiant City comes closest to what Wright intended. Wright made a serious effort to grapple with the housing problems of a decentralized, self-sufficient society, and even if he did not solve all of its problems, at least he openly acknowledged them.

Rosenbaum has done well to bring to light Wright's relationship to Henry Ford and what he speculates Ford may have had in mind when he pursued his own utopian vision, a wellspring for the Broadacre plan. Not least, the ideas underlying Broadacre City enlarge our ideas of the Taliesin Fellowship, Hillside Home School, and Wright's relationship to contemporary regionalist expressions.

INTRODUCTION

Usonia was Frank Lloyd Wright's vision for America, a place where design commingled with nature, expanding the idea of architecture to include a civilization, a utopian ideal that integrated spiritual harmony and material prosperity across a seamless, unspoiled landscape. Usonia was a state of mind, combining an evolving prescription for the elimination of high-density American cities and their replacement by pastoral communities organized around modern transportation and communications technology with a new type of home for middle-income families.

The Usonian house was relatively small when measured in square feet, but it was open and spacious, with access to the outside from almost every room. It was heated by warm water flowing through pipes embedded in a concrete slab. Usonian houses had no attic or basement; garages became carports. Light fixtures and much of the furniture were built in, simply part of the architecture. The walls were thin curtain walls, pre-fabricated board-and-batten sandwiches of plywood. The flat roof was supported by steel beams between masonry masses, which also housed kitchen, laundry, and other utilities.

One of the many hundred designs completed by Wright over his career was a Usonian house built for the Rosenbaum family in Florence, Alabama, in 1940. The clients were my parents, Stanley and Mildred (Mimi) Rosenbaum. It was the house where I grew up and is still the house where my mother lives. As a prototype Usonian house, the Rosenbaum residence provides an excellent introduction to Wright's efforts to create a small, low-cost house that could be replicated across the country.

I have often been asked what it was like to grow up in a Frank Lloyd Wright house. Unlike my parents, I had no basis for comparison with other experiences, since the house was already nearly five years old when I was born. It is also difficult to separate the contribution of my parents, the clients, from that of the architect. And even beyond their meeting of minds, the natural setting of the house, the surrounding neighborhood, town, area, and region were all important. Capturing a moment in history, the spirit of the times, the back-drop of politics, events, even movies are essential to understanding what it was like.

The experience of Usonian living can be felt at Taliesin or in any number of Wright houses that have been maintained in the manner intended. The Rosenbaum house makes its first impression from afar, seen over the rise of a hill, in the foreground with the Tennessee River a mile beyond to the south. In the afternoon sun the colors of the house are vivid: Cherokee red roof and brick and honey cypress, with surrounding greenery, mostly juniper and holly. The architect Paul Rudolph is said to have called the Rosenbaum living room "one of the most sublime spaces in American architecture," an impression that has remained with him since he first saw the room a half-century ago. My own memory picture is of Mimi playing "Moonlight Sonata" on the Baldwin, Stanley down in his study working out a Double-Crostic puzzle in the back of his weekly *Saturday Review of Literature*, the afternoon light filtered through the perforated boards under the eaves, making patterns on the floor. Dinner was prepared in a tiny kitchen just beyond the living room ("built like a galley in a Pullman car, where they prepare hundreds of meals a day from a similar-sized space," was how Stanley Rosenbaum used to explain it to visitors, as Frank Lloyd Wright had explained it to him). I also remember a Wright-designed console radio in the living room and imagine Stanley lurking to catch the latest war news on short-wave from Europe, and I remember the family gathered on the floor late at night for the Academy Awards, a special event for the family's movie theater business.

Playing with my brothers, David, Jonathan, and Michael, I constructed tunnels between ottomans and beneath blankets in our dormitory. Outside, our collie Diana lived in a Frank Lloyd Wright–inspired doghouse, with two rooms and a flat roof, constructed down the hill next to the barbecue pit, where we once briefly kept a goat, then rabbits. During the late 1940s two big elms came down, to be replaced by a spreading magnolia that I helped to plant in 1951, now huge and flowering.

An architecture critic for the *New York Times* saw a photograph of the cantilevered carport of the Rosenbaum house at the Museum of Modern Art in 1940 and compared it to a "great bird in flight."

As an adult I now experience the house as my mother's place, an extension of her personality and her relationship to a community that adopted her in the late 1930s when she moved to Florence from New York City after her wedding. Mimi Rosenbaum's house is one of craft and music, of artful arrangement, of beauty. While I was growing up, I experienced the house at least as much as my father's place, a realm for his ideas and intentions. Perhaps my perspective is also shaped by fond memories of my father's father and his houses, first across the street and then across town, large, typical brick and stucco dwellings that could not have been more different from our Wright-inspired style of living.

In and around Florence there were perhaps three kinds of houses: solid mansions and smaller houses made of brick; wooden houses with clapboards and wide porches, often occupied by families who rented; and unpainted, dogtrot shacks with tin roofs, usually set well off the road, insubstantial, seemingly temporary places for tenants who grew cotton and vegetables. The Rosenbaum house did not fit into any of these categories, but synthesized qualities of all three. At the edge of town on the threshold of the countryside, the house is not part of either the country or the town, but it relates to both.

Rosenbaum family portrait, 1954. Left to right: Stanley, David, Alvin, Jonathan, Michael, Mildred

From the outside, our Usonian is a wisp of a place, low and unobtrusive, made mostly of wood and tarpaper. Embedded into its landscape, it could also be imagined as existing on wheels, as movable as a car on the road, ready to settle into a different site someplace else. In many ways it is unimpressive, even insubstantial. But from the inside looking out it is solid. The house's three large masonry masses and four fireplaces give it a timeless sense, a sense that it has always been there and should never change. Because of Wright's reputation and the place my grandfather and father held in the community before the house was built, it also was endowed with prestige, a place to bring visitors, to show off, to talk about. Its picture appeared not only in books on Frank Lloyd Wright, but also in the Florence Chamber of Commerce brochure.

The inner life of the Rosenbaum house of the 1950s was its books and its people, not its shape or materials. The books that line the walls in every room act as a frame to a house that has no frame, making sturdy what otherwise might appear flimsy. As a meeting place, the house was often filled with people who had ideas and with the assertion of their ideals. As an intellectual and the town's only Harvard College graduate, Stanley Rosenbaum loaned out books, told stories, answered questions, and delighted in seeming to know everything. He could read literature in nearly a dozen languages and never stopped learning new things. The house and Stanley brought out the best impulses of out-of-town visitors who were often surprised to find liberal, enlightened, and informed conversation in a place like Florence, Alabama, in those days.

The inner life of the structure itself is in its craft, the details that turned its carpentry into art, lending a substance to Wright's form that exists as a tribute to the workers who built it. Time now speaks to the idea of preservation of this house that encouraged mind journeys into other cultures, a magnet for a constant stream of admirers, a house that in its conception was a prototype for an inexpensive, mass-produced, all-American dwelling for everyman, yet served as a friendly context for a family to find its own personality.

In sum my childhood homestead was a series of delightful contradictions: urbanity comfortably set into down-home informality; an architecture molded to our family and to its site, yet somehow reaching beyond, created by Wright as a model for an ideal design for living; and a southern community that accepted, indeed, celebrated, what appeared to others to be the incongruity of it all.

The house presents an opportunity to understand Wright the planner along with Wright the designer. The sensibility that Wright called Usonia was more than an architecture; it was an alternative design for

As with many Wright houses, the "front" of the Rosenbaum house was actually the back, facing the garden, with the Tennessee River beyond. This 1940 photograph was made by G. E. Kidder Smith for the Museum of Modern Art only a few days after the Rosenbaums had moved in.

nonurban, decentralized living given shape in the 1930s, first in his Broadacre plan and later in his Usonian houses. A bird's eye would see the Rosenbaum house as a section of Broadacre City, its many-layered red sand roof like a landscape in plan, flat as the prairie, rimmed by terrace-highways that provided access to each room-zone of our house-city. In the house, the interplay between one bedroom off a hallway of bedrooms and those bedrooms' relationship to indoor and outdoor communal areas suggest in their simplicity the spirit of the Broadacre City scheme and correspond to the components of decentralized places like Muscle Shoals. As a child I can remember closing my bedroom door when I wanted to be alone; then opening the door to the outside, slipping out onto the terrace and into the air, taking a walk into the neighborhood, or even to downtown Florence, half a mile away. After a while, I would go home, reentering the house through my bedroom. No one knew I had been out. I was able to assert my independence without announcing my intentions, without worrying my parents. In Florence I could walk from one end of town to the other in less than an hour, or bicycle to my elementary school in fifteen minutes. The streets were safe and mostly quiet. The people I passed knew who I was and who my parents were and where I was likely to be going, permitting me to be alone and with others at the same time.

The town of Florence and its sister towns of Sheffield and Tuscumbia—an amalgam known as Muscle Shoals—are nestled in the Tennessee Valley, in an area that was part of a grand scheme proposed by Henry Ford in the 1920s and realized in the 1930s as a regional development under the banner of the Tennessee Valley Authority. In some sense the Rosenbaum house, Muscle Shoals, and the Tennessee Valley provided a setting for the realization of Frank Lloyd Wright's vision, even though only the house can be traced directly to his hand.

Growing up in a Usonian house created a series of encounters that always seemed somehow connected, as if the architecture flavored everything that flowed through it or came near it, an aroma and taste experienced by nearly every passerby, to visitors, and among our family. It is a quality to which the integration of forms and textures, the prospects from the inside looking out, the ripple of levels down a gently sloping site, the materials and the craft of their joinery and finish, the extraordinary range of spaces—open and closed, dark and light, high and low, rough and smooth—all contribute.

This view of downtown Florence, Alabama, 1940, by Farm Security Administration photographer Arthur Rothstein, includes the Rosenbaums' Majestic Theater.

I had wanted to be an architect from early childhood, taking art lessons, designing with kraft paper, asking questions. Yet our house was distinctive not simply by a style of design, but by engendering a way of living that was wrapped in political discussion at the dinner table, in the books our father read to us from his vast library that lined the walls throughout the house, and in music and the movies. When a mouse or a cricket or even a garden snake was found inside, there was always a joke about "Mr. Wright letting the outside in," as if the wilderness itself were meant to creep across our threshold. With a carpeted concrete pad virtually level with the lawn in every room, the sensation of living in a Usonian house was that of living in the country without being part of it, of living close to the ground, but in comfort, not in the rough.

The connections in my mind between Usonian houses and the American story began, perhaps, with seeing other Frank Lloyd Wright houses and buildings on family trips during the 1950s, with visits to the Shavins in Chattanooga, the Kaufmann family at Bear Run, the Rebhuhns in Great Neck, and others. All different, all similar, as Wright adapted his designs to site and surround, yet imbued each place with an American sensibility that connected Alabama with Wisconsin, California with Virginia. My home town, Florence, was not isolated in this place that Wright called Usonia. Learning about Wright led to a brief stint as an apprentice at Taliesin and a continuing interest in Wright's buildings, writings, and influence on American design. At Taliesin I was surprised at the additional powerful effect of Wright-inspired design when experienced as a complete environment, rather than simply within a household. Life at Taliesin West in 1965, when I was in residence, amid the color of the desert rocks and cacti, the surprising flowering plants, everything set into a workaday context by the compound of buildings, the grove of citrus, the view of the Paradise Valley, the table settings and the discussions at dinner, the musicales, the work in the drafting room, the eternal youth of an esprit de corps fed by Wright's "truth against the world"—everything conspired to lend substance to Wright's words in books, another layer of understanding to his buildings, including the one where I was raised.

As I looked for evidence of a Usonian sensibility, it seemed to be part of a larger culture that had survived the 1930s. I found Usonia in the politics of Adlai Stevenson, the music of Aaron Copland, the magazine layouts of Alexander Lieberman, and the photographs of Walker Evans. My impressions of Usonia were also colored by Muscle Shoals. If Muscle Shoals was the center of my own Usonia, was it also a special place to Frank Lloyd Wright? As I delved into the literature on Usonian architecture and Broadacre City and Wright's speeches, correspondence, and other papers, I was astonished to learn that Wright, indeed, was specifically and energetically enthusiastic about Muscle Shoals as a model for Usonia and Broadacre City as early as 1930. He had been intrigued by plans promoted by Henry Ford in the early 1920s to turn Muscle Shoals into a decentralized, industrialized "75 Mile City," a regional plan incorporating housing, commercial, industrial, recreational, cultural, and educational facilities along a 75-mile stretch of the Tennessee River, beginning at Seven-Mile Island at the bend of the river near Florence and stretching east to Huntsville. Later, when Franklin Roosevelt made Muscle Shoals the birthplace of the New Deal by making it the headquarters for the Tennessee Valley Authority—the first piece of New Deal legislation to pass Congress in 1933—Wright followed closely and applauded this federal development that promoted regional, nonurban planning. When my parents contacted Frank Lloyd Wright through an architect friend in 1939, Muscle Shoals and TVA were prominently mentioned.

The Broadacre City idea and the reality of Muscle Shoals seemed curiously in tune. Like Broadacre City, Muscle Shoals and Florence had an American character that superseded the region. Florence was more progressive and more giving than most southern places its size. As I probed, I found mounting evidence that the tenets of Wright's Usonia—an architecture of natural materials in sympathy with the environment—were combined with principles that included a number of ideas considered progressive during the first quarter of the 20th century, including automobility and electrification, equal rights for women, the role of experts in government planning, decentralization, the celebration of American arts and letters, experimental education and respect for the individual. Usonia served to integrate a range of issues across all of American civilization into Wright's credo, a single principle that could influence work, family, and civic life as well as delineate space. Further investigations revealed that Usonia did not spring forth as a full-blown prescription at once, but evolved from principles that Wright enunciated as early as 1900, ideas that grew in his practice of architecture, in his writings, and as he conducted his life.

Professor Elizabeth Walter, art department chair at the University of North Alabama, was first to record the connection between Ford and TVA, Wright's Broadacre City, and the Rosenbaum house. Writing in 1982, Walter observed that "the curious circumstances of site and location may have prompted [Wright] to associate the commission with the very model [in Broadacre City] that had occupied his thoughts for so long a time." Stanley Rosenbaum speculated for years on the connections between Henry Ford and Frank Lloyd Wright, but it was Walter who found many of the actual links between

Henry Ford at Muscle Shoals, Alabama, 1921

Ford's proposal of 1922 for Muscle Shoals and the Broadacre City concept, which Wright began to publicize in 1930. The series of experiments to optimize production efficiencies in the manufacture of the Model T that Ford carried out in his Michigan village industries before World War I led to his Muscle Shoals proposals and influenced plans for the creation of the Tennessee Valley Authority during Franklin Roosevelt's first hundred days as president. The concepts behind these schemes flowed directly into the models for Wright's Broadacre City and later into the design, construction methods, siting, and location of his Usonian houses, as well as their social assumptions.

Wright's facility as an artist and architect of dwellings and his ability as an integrator of social, intellectual, and political trends have not always been adequately delineated. His contributions to planning and to the American way of life are often submerged beneath his extraordinary ability to create beautiful houses harmonious with nature, his sense of romance and music in design, and a reputation in the forefront of America's artistic history.

This book is about the sensibility Wright called Usonia and the clients who helped define it. It is also about the people and events that had an influence on Wright, with and without his acknowledgment, and the people and events he influenced, wittingly and unwittingly. In the literal sense Usonia was unrealized. In another sense it took form in the late 1930s in the Rosenbaum house and its environment. And after World War II many of its elements would emerge in the automobile suburb, the ubiquitous ranch-style house of increasingly prefabricated construction with a carport and sliding glass doors onto a patio surrounded by natural landscaping, and a dozen other little things that, in becoming standard, have become invisible.

1. UNITY

The science of printing is to make the book a medium of human expression
more facile than building and the book is to become a means of recording life
perhaps more enduring than the great edifice ever was.
—Frank Lloyd Wright, 1953

Frank Lloyd Wright's informal education was a stream of books, conversation, and lectures by speakers who made the circuit to places like Madison, Wisconsin. From the beginning he was enthralled by new ideas, captivated by the spiritual, and possessed by an insatiable curiosity about complex systems and the orchestration of their parts.

Beyond his immediate family, Wright was devoted to the Lloyd-Joneses, his mother's family, who were important in his early education. They included a close-knit circle of aunts, uncles, and cousins that surrounded him in Madison and at their nearby rural homestead. According to his sister, Maginel Wright Barney, the Lloyd-Joneses were "honorable people, devoted to education, to nature, to the Unitarian Church and to each other. They were splendid people, high-minded, possibly high-handed too, now and then," known by those who lived around them as "the God-Almighty Joneses." Besides his mother, Anna, the person who probably had the greatest influence on Wright was his patriarchal Uncle Jenkin Lloyd-Jones, a Unitarian minister whose long white beard gave him a resemblance to Walt Whitman. Each summer, the Reverend Lloyd-Jones would direct a tent assembly near Madison or Spring Green, a Unitarian Chautauqua with speakers who included future Wisconsin governor and U.S. senator Robert La Follette, who came each year; settlement house founder Jane Addams; and suffragette Susan B. Anthony.

Wright was only a notch younger than the generation who joined the Progressive party in politics, and he was swept up into the movement, which was centered on his home turf of Madison and his adopted city of

Frank Lloyd Wright, c. 1904

Chicago. Editor William Allen White described his fellow Progressives as "well-to-do farmers, skilled artisans, small businessmen, professional men, upper brackets of organized labor, successful middle-class country-town citizens, the country editor, the well-paid engineer." Socially minded ministers like Jenkin Lloyd-Jones preached that concern for one's fellow man was part of the national purpose. The movement was led into the mainstream by the youthful Theodore Roosevelt and Robert La Follette and included their contemporaries Frederick Jackson Turner, also from Wisconsin; John Dewey and Thorstein Veblen at the University of Chicago; Jane Addams at Hull House; and Woodrow Wilson at Princeton. William Jennings Bryan served as a gadfly, representing rural, traditional values, but in search of essentially the same political results. Their mission, in part, was to expand social services through the introduction of experts into the processes of government, including the establishment of a professional civil service concerned with human welfare rather than personal gain. Coming of age in the 1890s, Progressives turned the populism of their elders into a new force for reform.

The young Wright's world was changing with breathtaking speed: Engines were replacing muscle in factories; cities were overflowing with new arrivals from the countryside and new immigrants from Europe; small enterprise was being engulfed by big business. In the midst of these transformations social reformers, visionaries, and muckraking journalists forged a spirited and popular alliance with farmers and other rural conservatives. For Progressives like Robert La Follette and Theodore Roosevelt, it was the individual that counted. Their leadership gave a voice to those who sought their own way, whose ideas could give shape to progress and to Progressive ideals, including intellectuals and artists like Wright.

Under La Follette (who served as governor from 1900 to 1906 and as U.S. senator from 1906 to 1925), Wisconsin pioneered the use of hydroelectric power and the effective regulation of public utilities and promoted conservation, scientific agriculture, income and inheritance taxes, workmen's compensation, social security, and a dozen other reforms that found their way into New Deal programs in the 1930s. They would also find their way into Wright's ideas for Usonia and Broadacre City. William Jennings Bryan's populism later influenced and was influenced by Henry Ford, whose ideas would in turn have tremendous influence on Wright. Wright would develop ideas sympathetic with the Progressive causes of reform, modernization, a better economic balance between cities and rural areas, equality between the sexes, and curbing the excesses of the ruling class and providing opportunities for those less fortunate. For the politicians and academics, the concerns were social and economic while for Wright they were architectural; but their agendas overlapped to a considerable degree.

While it is not known whom young Frank Lloyd Wright met at his Uncle Jenkin's meetings or across the dinner table, it is clear that he read constantly. In later life he observed that the "book fodder for which we have a natural taste does most to feed the thing we call ourselves." A boyhood reading list that he prepared for *Scholastic* magazine in 1932 suggests an early fascination with far-off places and pastoral settings such as those in *Arabian Nights Entertainments*, *Gulliver's Travels*, and *Robinson Crusoe*. As a student, Wright read Horatio Greenough, Henry David Thoreau, and Victor Hugo, remembering particularly "This Will Kill That," a chapter in Hugo's *Notre Dame de Paris* (1831), which he later called "the best amateur essay on architecture ever published." While still in short pants Wright came upon Hugo's idea that the Renaissance was the end of architecture. Until Gutenberg's time, Hugo wrote, "Architecture was the principal, universal form of writing...[the cathedral, a] gigantic book of stone." The artists of the Romanesque and Gothic cathedrals were not the priests, but the architects who created hundreds of epic churches across Europe, covering walls with inscriptions, telling stories in stained-glass windows, sculpture, and painting. The invention of movable type and the spread of God's word through the book killed the cathedral.

For Wright the lesson was clear. His artistic ideas were best conveyed in his buildings but could also take form in writing. Over his life his enormous output would include correspondence, books, articles, newsletters, broadsides, brochures, and lectures, as well as designs for houses and other building types, furniture, cars, airplanes, graphics, cocktail glasses, appliances, objets d'art, textiles, lamps, fixtures, and hardware, and, at the other end of the scale, grand schemes for developments, neighborhoods, cities, and whole regions. The ideas that framed Usonia—Broadacre City and the Usonian house—would emerge first as word-images, then would be translated into abstract forms still supported more by language than pictures, then followed by a set of principles, and would only later take shape as an architecture realized in wood, brick, glass, and concrete. This integration of focused, thematic design-ideas with discourse sets Wright apart from virtually every other 19th- and 20th-century artist.

Wright's first association with a publishing venture was in 1897 in the creation of a book, *The House Beautiful*, by William C. Gannett, a Unitarian minister, friend and colleague of Wright's uncle Jenkin. The project was a backyard private press affair, printed by hand by Wright's first independent client, William Herman Winslow, behind his now-famous River Forest, Illinois, house. Wright provided the

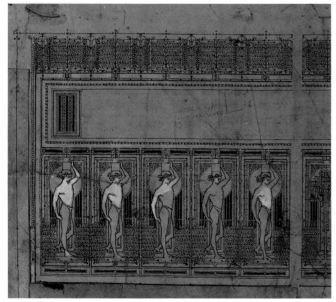

The House Beautiful, title page (detail), 1897

page decorations. While drawings and photographs of Wright's architecture were published as early as 1887, his first written publications appeared in 1900 and 1901: a brief introduction to an exhibition catalog of Japanese prints and two lectures. The first lecture was "The Architect," given before a meeting of the Architectural League of America, in Chicago in June 1900, attacking the architect as a servant to capitalists who "pander[s] to silly women his artistic sweets.' His second published speech, "The Art and Craft of the Machine," first delivered at the Chicago Arts and Crafts Society at Hull House in March 1901 and later revised and delivered before other groups, was far more important, presenting his ideas for America's first native architecture as one that would combine appropriate technology and the honest use of materials. In these and in articles presenting "A Home in a Prairie Town" and "A Small House with 'Lots of Room in It,'" published around the same time in *Ladies' Home Journal*, Wright unfurled his flag as the architect of Hugo's prophecy. As the rising star of Chicago architecture, he used his newly gained access to an audience to promote his calling.

In his early publications a pattern emerged that would be characteristic of his written work and lectures. In a description of what he loved, the language is lilting and graceful, often elegant. The ideas expressed ring true, with a sincerity and spirit that is in sympathy with his work as an artist. By contrast Wright's criticism of what he loathed is neither lyrical nor profound, often drifting into polemics taken to the extremes of absurdity. Indeed, Wright's language of scorn, his bitter denunciations of New York, Pittsburgh, Milwaukee, Washington, European architects, rapacious landlords, the "mobocracy," bankers, and the rest sound coarse, the language unskilled, striking the shrill notes of a publicity seeker.

The darks and lights of Wright's art—subdued, cozy, cave-like rooms and corridors suddenly opening to great expanses, flooded with color and light—follow not only the rhythms of nature but ideas more ancient than Athens, the teachings of Lao-tzu. Wright acknowledged his debt to Lao-tzu and to the Tao, a philosophy in which discord defines harmony. Wright's vision was defined in space, seeking contrast to assert its place, a contrast that Grant Hildebrand has characterized in terms of landscape, as "prospect and refuge." This duality in his art found expression in words as the contrast of good and evil. As Wright's apprentice, Edgar Tafel, explained it, "every architectural episode in Mr. Wright's life had to have a villain."

Indeed, Wright learned his lesson well from his Lieber Meister Louis Sullivan, whose architectural villain eventually became a collection of temporary buildings constructed in Chicago's Jackson Park. "The damage wrought by the World's Fair will last for half a century from its date if not longer. It has penetrated deep into the constitution of the American mind, effecting there lesions significant of dementia," Sullivan observed in his autobiography thirty years after the fair.

Wright was working in Sullivan's office when the fair opened, a year late. The World's Columbian Exposition was promoted to commemorate the 400th anniversary of Columbus's voyage to America, but the organizers had problems securing a sufficient number of exhibitors, a consequence of the financial panic on Wall Street and an epidemic of bank failures. The gates swung open in early May 1893, and Frank Lloyd Wright, among the crowds, inspected Daniel Burnham's Great White Way. "Just half a century earlier," Henry Steele Commager wrote, "[Horatio Greenough] had been rebuked for his figure of George Washington in a toga...[now it was logical that] American statesmen and diplomats should all have worn togas to match the

World's Columbian Exposition, Chicago, Illinois, 1893, view from the Basin and the Electricity Building (left, foreground) to the Illinois Building (center, at the horizon). Japan's Ho-o-den was located on the Wooded Island across a lagoon from the Illinois Building.

post offices, banks, and other public buildings...." Wright agreed with Henry Adams, who viewed the fair as "the first expression of American thought as a unity." He also would have agreed with Adams's remark that the fair was "a step in evolution to startle Darwin," supported by patrons who "treated architecture as 'stage decoration.'"

Unity was achieved by the establishment of a uniform cornice height for the fair buildings and by a strict classical hegemony, rooted in Burnham's Swedenborgian sense that heaven was a pristine earth with beautiful cities, a perfect and perfectly organized society. Inside these perfect buildings were perfect exhibits, arranged in a careful system of classification by the Smithsonian's G. Brown Goode, an effort "to formulate the modern," as Goode quoted Walt Whitman in an explanation of his task. But perhaps even more important to the sense of unity that captured the nation's attention was Frederick Law Olmsted's landscape plan for the fair, which was essential to the creation of an idealized vision in picture postcards—a combination of the Washington Mall and the Disney World of its day.

From Wright's memory, as reported in his own *Autobiography*, and from other accounts of the scene, it is easy to imagine Wright's first day at the fair: he probably first toured the Transportation Building, a touch of Romanesque amid the orchestration of Beaux Arts classical revival and rococo. The structure's great golden archway was designed by Sullivan, but design of the building itself was dictated by Burnham's office and executed by S. S. Bemen on Adler and Sullivan's staff. Once inside, Wright may have lingered at a garden cafe on the mezzanine before strolling to the central court, where he undoubtedly studied the large-scale model of the "ideal" workers' community of Pullman, Illinois, the community had been constructed outside Chicago in 1880 as an experiment by the railroad sleeping car company, and Wright had undoubtedly visited there in the past.

After seeing Sullivan's great portal and the exhibits inside, Wright might have walked north along the lagoon, then across to the Midway, discovering elephants, gondolas, Greek statues, the original Ferris wheel, the "Ottoman's Arab Wild East Show." We know that, seeking higher-brow pleasures, he visited the Fine Arts Building, discovering the woodblock prints of Japanese artists Hokusai and Hiroshige. Reversing his course, he then crossed a bridge to find Japan's compound far from the hubbub on a wooded island in the lagoon and to admire the Ho-o-den, a half-scale replica of a temple dating from the time of the Fujiwara shoguns in the 11th century. This seemingly natural structure of woven straw and unpainted wood, screens of rice paper, and panels of plain plaster was the part of the fairyland most appealing to Wright, a peaceful place away from the babel, Little Egypt's hootchy-kootchy, and the blast of saxophones from Florenz Ziegfeld's big band revue.

Others who strolled through the White City that summer were eleven-year-old Franklin Delano Roosevelt; his uncle, railroad-executive-cum-regional-planner Frederic Delano; and Arthur Morgan, who, 40 years later, would be appointed by Roosevelt to help create the Tennessee Valley Authority.

The exposition was also the site of a variety of special events, including a "World's Congress of Historians and Historical Students," held inside the fairgrounds. Thirty-one-year-old University of Wisconsin professor Frederick Jackson Turner read his paper, "The Significance of the Frontier in American History," presenting ideas that were perhaps of greater importance than the fair itself. Turner concluded that the American frontier had been the source of "individualism...self-reliance...inventiveness...[and] the restless energy of the American character...." American democracy, said Turner, "came out of the forest, and it gained new strength each time it touched a new frontier." The fair's fakery, its classical piles of snowy white plaster palaces arranged in axial symmetry, represented the antithesis of Wright's training under Sullivan and of his own instincts, while Turner's thesis became Wright's religion. As Turner declared the closing of the frontier by the advance of the industrial juggernaut, Wright saw an opportunity to transform the hackneyed architecture of old Europe into a new sensibility that would grow out of the colors and vistas of the American landscape.

In 1893, at the age of 26, Wright had put a playhouse addition under construction at his Forest Avenue house in Oak Park, a Richardsonian shingle style residence he had completed in 1889. With his eldest son Lloyd a toddler, John less than a year old, and his wife, Catherine, pregnant with their third, Wright's domestic circle was already half-drawn. He had also completed another shingle-style building to house his aunts' Hillside Home School in Spring Green, Wisconsin. Apart from family projects, he had designed an ensemble of summer cottages, a retreat in a piney woods on the Gulf of Mexico at Ocean Springs, Mississippi, for Sullivan and his friends, including a cottage for James Charnley. That year Charnley also commissioned a Chicago town house from Sullivan, which Wright executed at Astor Place near Lake Michigan. It was the first of his designs that was characteristically Wrightian.

Wright's vision was formed in rough outline. The same year, 1893, he opened his own office, with small gold lettering stenciled on clear plate glass—FRANK LLOYD WRIGHT, ARCHITECT—on the 15th floor of the Schiller Building on Randolph Street. From 1893 to 1901 he designed 71 buildings, of which 49 were built. By the turn of the century, dwellings for his clients began to emerge "out of the ground and into the light," combining the serenity of safe places with the enthusiasm of discovery. He soon grew comfortable with the affluence of success and with a life that included a beautiful and loving wife from a prosperous family, an assembly of talented and handsome children, expensive motorcars and fine riding horses, frequent concerts, visits to fancy restaurants, a trip with friends to Japan, memberships in the Caxton Club (for rare book collectors), the Cliff

Como Orchard Summer Colony, Darby, Montana, 1910

Dwellers (a congenial dining club for artists and writers), and the Oak Park Tennis Club, participation in the Chicago Horse Show, additions to his home, expensive furnishings, rugs, and Oriental objets d'art, fine clothing, parties, and the support and services of a growing office and domestic staff.

From 1901 to 1909 Wright received more than 100 more commissions and completed nearly 70 buildings, including the E-Z Polish Factory; residences for Frederick Robie, Avery Coonley, Meyer May, Isabel Roberts, J. R. Ziegler, and dozens of others; and his first foray into the West, an ambitious site plan, cottages, lodges, and other buildings for the Como Orchard Summer Colony (also called University Heights) and a new town in the Bitter Root Valley of Montana. Wright's client for this first venture into town planning was Frederick Nicholas, a Chicago real estate developer, who was the promoter of both projects. Recent research by Australian scholar

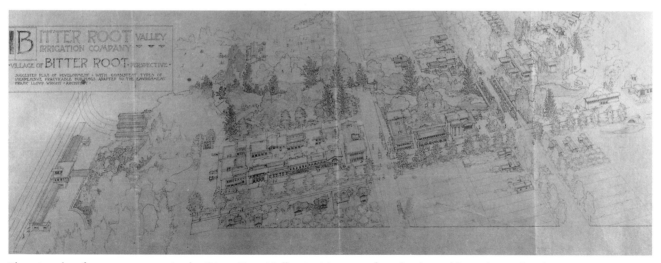

The site plan for a new town in the Bitter Root Valley in Montana foreshadowed Broadacre City by separating modes of transport and avoiding a town center, permitting the landscape of southern Montana to invade the town's grid.

Donald Leslie Johnson suggests that Bitter Root presaged Broadacre City in many important ways:

> The center of Bitter Root town was to be a great garden that lay before the inn. Bitter Root village and Broadacre City had no identifiable center or urban focus, just as the idea for Broadacre City was about regional decentralization, within the city there was to be further decentralization....The Bitter Root plan and Broadacre City were organized by a compelling geometry and proportional system. Functional location was assigned by Wright's perception of the dynamics and importance of transport—individual, commercial, and mass.

The Bitter Root plan separated pedestrian, vehicular, and rail systems and moved the major buildings to the town's edge. Like other projects of the era, Como Orchard and Bitter Root were encouraged by railroads, in this case the Union Pacific, to increase western settlement. (Years later, Averell Harriman, who served as the Union Pacific's chairman in the 1930s, successfully developed a similar project in Sun Valley, Idaho.)

In 1909 Wright became dissatisfied with his life. Material success, marriage, and fatherhood had carried him far away from an artist's life, imposing a constant burden of middle-class responsibilities against which he increasingly rebelled. Following in his father's footsteps, 42-year-old Wright left his family, abandoning a good reputation and a considerable number of works in progress. Later he explained in his *Autobiography*: "I was losing grip on my work and even my interest in it…. Because I did not know what I wanted I wanted to go away." Curiously, in explaining his anguish over leaving his work and his family, Wright blamed the automobile: "Ever since boyhood [I had loved] horseback riding, swimming, dancing, skating and omnivorous reading...[and] music..." when "Motoring (just that much added or was it deducted?) had come along to interfere with these recreations...[bringing] a disturbance to all values, subtle and obvious, and [bringing] disturbance to me."

On September 22, 1909, he left town on the spur of the moment, after collecting client fees and selling as many Japanese prints as possible one morning before boarding a train for a rendezvous with 30-year-old Mamah Borthwick Cheney, the mother of two and wife to Wright's client, Edwin Cheney. The following day they met in New York and sailed for London, then went on to Berlin, where Wright had received an offer from the publisher Ernst Wasmuth to issue a large portfolio of his work.

When they arrived in England, the newspaper headlines were announcing passage by the British parliament of the South Africa Act, a reorganization of Capetown, Natal, the Transvaal, and the Orange River Colony into one state under the British crown, a new nation called the Union of South Africa, or U.S.A. It has been suggested that Wright first thought of the word "Usonia," a euphonious acronym for the United States of North America, at that time, to distinguish the United States from the Union of South Africa. He later attributed the word to Samuel Butler's utopian novel *Erehwon* (although it does not appear there or anywhere else in Butler's works). Wright's first uses of the word were in his 1923 manifesto against the skyscraper, *Experimenting with Human Lives*, and in a 1925 article in the Dutch architecture magazine *Wendingen*. He later explained: "The 'United States' did not appear to [Butler] a good title for us as a nation and the word 'American' belonged to us only in common with a dozen or more countries. So he suggested USONIAN—roots of the word in the word unity or in union. This seemed to me appropriate. So I have often used this word when needing reference to our own country or style."

During his European hegira, Wright, joined by his son Lloyd, shuttled between a Berlin apartment and a

Despite Wright's reduced circumstances after his return from Europe, he designed and began to build a vast complex on the Wisconsin landscape, a home that he refined and rebuilt over the next half century. The living quarters of the 1911 structure were destroyed by fire in 1914; other parts of the structure survive in today's Taliesin.

cream-white villa on the Via Verdi outside Florence. For a year he worked, took time off, and visited museums. In 1910 he returned to Oak Park and Catherine, leaving Mamah Cheney behind. A few months later she returned to file for a divorce from Cheney and reclaim her Frank. Through this domestic upheaval, Wright began to build a new home, Taliesin, in Spring Green, Wisconsin, on land provided by his family, where he finally settled in with his mother and mistress on Christmas 1911, scandalizing the locals.

Through this midlife crisis, Frank Lloyd Wright's self-image underwent an apparent change, from that of a respectable Chicago professional to that of a rebel in exile, "persecuted...pursued and exploited by publicity." Writing his *Autobiography* in the late 1920s, a period when he had no work or prospect for work, he reflected on this period of his life defensively, seeing himself as a victim of circumstance and culture. In fact he had become the toast of Europe and was tremendously influential among his professional colleagues in Chicago. His complaint was then (and later) that his admirers were merely imitators without knowledge, sensitivity, or understanding of the cause of organic architecture, that they reduced his original ideas to "fictitious semblances."

Now in seclusion, folded into a southern Wisconsin hillside, Wright remained a source of inspiration and a distant figure of admiration, his work routinely published, his contributions to architecture regularly praised. Nevertheless, he declared in the May 1914 issue of *Architectural Record*: "Alone in my field the cause was unprofitable, seemingly impossible, almost unknown, or, ...as a rule, unhonored and ridiculed." In a close study of this period, biographer Robert Twombly characterized Wright's manifesto as "his first proclamation of the 'persecuted genius' legend, the interpretation of his life as a continuous battle against overwhelming odds, a struggle for principle despite social ostracism, professional ignorance, financial loss, ridicule, and rejection." To these were added tragedy. In early August 1914, Wright was at lunch with his son John when word arrived that Taliesin had been set ablaze. Together with Mamah Borthwick's former husband, Edwin Cheney, they made their way to Spring Green, finding Borthwick, her two children, and four others dead, victims of a murderous rampage by Wright's chef, who had set the fire.

During this period of change and loss, Wright designed three projects that are early examples of his integrated approach to design: Taliesin (1911; rebuilt after the fire in 1914), Midway Gardens in Chicago (1913), and the Imperial Hotel in Tokyo (1915). For all of these Wright not only controlled the design of the building but imagined site, structure, decoration, fixtures, and furniture as a whole, a single story writ large, its purpose and form unified into one grand gesture.

All three of Wright's great buildings of the era were conceived as retreats from the workaday world. At Taliesin, Wright literally escaped from middle-class Oak Park into a Shangri-la of his own making, an aerie of his ancestors offering comforting seclusion and protection. Midway Gardens was also a retreat, a garden resort near the site of the 1893 Exposition that replaced the fakery of Renaissance facades and honky-tonk excess with an elegant Prairie Style expanse of outdoor terraces, promenades, loggias, and gardens for concerts, dances, and performances, a complex with restaurants and lounges tucked into corners and behind long, open-air galleries.

With its interplay of outdoor and indoor spaces, Midway Gardens arrived, according to Henry-Russell Hitchcock, "at a richness and complexity of architectural form only prepared for in earlier work....[with]

sculpture and paintings designed by Wright [that] parallel the most advanced forms of European painters, barely known at this time in America through the Armory Show." Like Midway, Tokyo's official hotel for foreign visitors was conceived on a grand scale, its layout like an English garden maze: guests emerged from a labyrinth of long, low hallways into light-filled atria, encountering, in a sudden turn, pools of water lilies edged with evergreen bonsai, then an arcade, lobby, or cabaret. From carpeting to furniture, from the shape

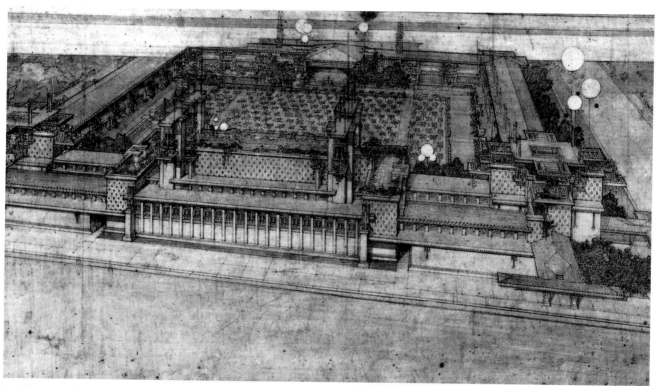

Building Midway Gardens (1913) must have been sweet revenge for Wright, who created this entertainment center on a site near the grounds of the World's Columbian Exposition. An insensitive proprietor and then Prohibition destroyed Midway, which was finally demolished in 1929.

of its enormous bathtubs to the fortress-like garden walls that shielded the hotel's guests from the hustle of jinrikshas and the crowds on the Ginza a few blocks away, the Imperial, like Midway Gardens, integrated the smallest details of design with larger considerations: the relationship of the building to the surrounding gardens and then of architecture and landscaping with site, neighborhood, and city. From its subterranean earthquake-proof footings to its lava rock fountains, from its bathrooms to its teacups, each of the Imperial's interlocking details informed another, forming a vast complex that was perceivable as an intelligible whole only when viewed as a plan from the architect's drawings. Wright's insistence on orchestration of the whole in these projects anticipates the essence of Usonia: the establishment of architectural hegemony by the creation of a sensibility, indeed, a whole society, based on the precepts of organic architecture.

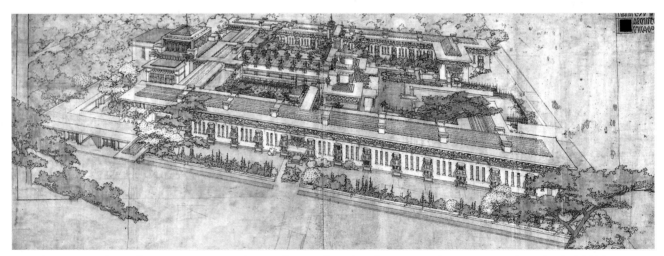

Wright's Imperial Hotel (1915) was complete to the smallest detail. It survived a major earthquake (1923) but not Toyko's soaring land values. The Imperial was demolished in 1968. The entrance lobby was saved and reconstructed at Meiji Village near Nagoya, Japan, in 1976.

2. MUSCLE SHOALS

When Wright left Oak Park in 1909 he left his architectural practice in the hands of Herman V. von Holst, a Chicago architect of little talent but formidable business skills and social connections. He selected von Holst presumably for these reasons and on the condition that he hire Wright's assistants to perform the design work. One of these was the talented Marion Mahony, Illinois's first practicing woman architect, who had previously worked for von Holst. The contract between von Holst and Wright, signed on the day Wright left for Europe, stated, "Compensation for all work at hand, or probable or prospective...is to be divided equally between them," with twenty specific projects listed as being under construction, probable and prospective, or as work in hand. One of the projects not listed on the contract was a prospective commission for a house for Henry and Clara Ford of Dearborn, Michigan.

While considerable confusion exists over when and where Wright met Henry Ford, it is clear that Ford visited Wright to discuss a project with him. Probably the best account of the event is from Grant Manson, who conducted a lengthy 1940 interview with John van Bergan, who was on duty in Frank Lloyd Wright's studio when Henry Ford came calling, only a few days before Wright left for Europe. "He remembers [the] visit from Ford," wrote Manson, "and Wright's inability to maintain his customary, self-confident manner."

According to Donald Leslie Johnson, the commission was given to Wright in 1909 along with a commission from Ford's design chief, Childe Harold Wills. Von Holst took over both the Ford and Wills commissions, and Mahony designed a house for Ford in 1912, as well as a house for Wills. The Wills project was never started, but the foundations were laid for the Ford house. During the summer of 1913 the *Detroit News-Tribune* published an item stating that the Chicago architecture firm of von Holst & Fyfe were designing a marble mansion in Dearborn for Ford at a cost of $2 million. Ford confirmed that he would build in Dearborn, but denied that he would spend lavishly: "What on earth would I do with a palace like that?" he complained. Henry Ford, his contractor, and the architect quarreled. Ford abandoned von Holst for W. H. Van Tine, an obscure interior decorator living in Pittsburgh, who redesigned the house but used the existing foundations, more or less. Von Holst sued Ford. In an out-of-court settlement of fees made on July 23, 1915, Ford paid von Holst the enormous sum of $22,500 (nearly $500,000 in today's dollars).

The resulting house, Fair Lane, is an ungainly Gothic pile on a large, beautiful tract of land on the banks of the River Rouge that was later landscaped by Jens Jensen. The only part of the house containing a sugges-

The surviving elements of a Prairie School sensibility at Henry and Clara Ford's Fair Lane include the swimming pool wing (far right), which may have been designed by Marion Mahony, and the grounds, designed by Wright's friend and sometime collaborator, landscape architect Jens Jensen.

tion of Marion Mahony's design is the indoor swimming pool, which was built for Edsel, Henry and Clara Ford's son. A course of clerestory windows under a wide eaves with a distinctive soffit decoration is clearly in the Prairie School style. The elder Fords never used the pool. E. G. Liebold, Ford's personal assistant at the time, speculated that "Edsel might have discussed Frank Lloyd Wright [with his father] as the designer of the residence." Wright never acknowledged the Ford commission, perhaps out of embarrassment at having abandoned an important project to von Holst, only to see the job botched several years later.

Wright would later meet Edsel Ford on more than one occasion, including a visit to Ford's River Rouge factory around 1920. More interesting, though, is a possible vicarious connection with Henry Ford through Jenkin Lloyd-Jones, who, as an outspoken pacifist, joined Ford's isolationist campaign against U.S. involvement in World War I. Lloyd-Jones and his wife Edith accompanied Ford, 52 other crusaders, and 47 journalists on a highly publicized Christmas peace mission to Scandinavia in 1915. Wright was close to his elderly uncle and identified with his causes. But most important, Wright would later acknowledge Ford's contribution to the development of his own ideas.

In 1893, the year Wright opened his office in Chicago, Ford road tested his first automobile in Detroit. By 1909, when Wright first met Ford, the Model T had been launched, placing the ownership of an automobile within reach of every American family (15 million Model T Fords were sold before they were discontinued in 1928, with new models selling for as little as $300). The countryside was radically changed by the automobile in an era that was generally prosperous. "There was never a time when the American farmer was as well off as he is today," pronounced Theodore Roosevelt after receiving a report from his Commission on Country

Life in 1909. At first the automobile upset rural life. Motorized carriages competed with horses for right of way on the roads. New taxes were proposed. To most people who lived in the country, motoring was a leisure activity for rich city slickers, not poor farmers.

But as the Model T spread and farm-to-market roads improved, opposition to the automobile began to fade. In 20 years the automobile went from being an extravagance for the privileged few to a necessity for virtually everyone in America not living in New York City. Rural life grew more complex. But cities still provided distinct advantages—better jobs, better schools, recreation, and modern conveniences—and so drew migration from the farms. To stop the influx into urban areas, jobs had to be created in the countryside that would reverse the trend. Henry Ford and the Populists and Frank Lloyd Wright and the Progressives all recognized the need to bring the prosperity of the city to the country without undermining the benefits of country life.

While industry was slow to make the move, modern conveniences help to stem the tide. As Henry Ford remarked: "A very decided drift away from the farms was checked by three elements—the cheap automobile, the good roads over which the farmer might travel to market, [and] the moving picture theater in the community where the farmer and his family might enjoy an evening's entertainment." The parallel flowering of Ford's Model T and Thomas Edison's movies gave Americans mobility, one by locomotion, the other by flights into fantasy. In short, they both offered escape, even outside urban centers, from what was humdrum, difficult, or unpleasant.

During the same period, the problems of cities—congestion, crime, dirt, and ugliness—stimulated thinkers and poets, social planners, and critics to look to the horizon for solutions. The first Chicago trolley suburb, Lake Forest, was laid out in 1856, in a picturesque manner—curving roads, edged by lawns and trees—followed by Riverside, designed by Olmsted and Vaux in 1868, a decade after their work on Central Park in New York. More important, rebuilding after the great fire of 1871 transformed downtown Chicago into America's first exclusively commercial district, casting residential development out from the city center.

As Chicago and other cities were undergoing tremendous changes, the Wild West was being tamed by settlement. Frederick Jackson Turner, writing in *Atlantic Monthly* in September 1896, argued that the frontier experience made America not only different from Europe, but better. "Out of the freedom of his opportunities, [the pioneer] fashioned a formula for social regeneration—the freedom of the individual to seek his own...." Democracy was a product of the wilderness, not of city life. By the turn of the century, the call of the wild seized the public imagination. The books of Jack London, Rudyard Kipling, and Edgar Rice Burroughs became best sellers. Theodore Roosevelt, flexing his muscles in adventures abroad, preached that Americans should lead a "life of strenuous endeavor," proclaiming that we needed "a greater and not less[er] development of the fundamental frontier virtues."

The tension between the benefits of rural and city life grew as technology entered people's lives. In houses built in cities and towns, electric lights, telephone service, and plumbing provided conveniences not found in the country, while the automobile provided the mobility to find an escape into the countryside from the perceived ills of urban existence. With webs of intersecting roads for automobility and webs of high-voltage wiring for universal electrification, American regions began to merge. Remote places became accessible and pressures on urban areas found relief. Leading the way, Henry Ford and Thomas Edison converged on the Tennessee River Valley to imagine a new kind of community, a regional settlement of homes and industries far from the city.

■

The Tennessee River flows down from the Smoky Mountains in East Tennessee and North Carolina, across the top of Alabama from east to west, making a bend at Muscle Shoals, then heading north, back through Tennessee to Paducah, Kentucky, where it spills into the Ohio River. In the 19th century, the river was not navigable at Muscle Shoals. Passengers and goods would move by steamboat between Knoxville and Decatur, then required portage by rail, emerging at Florence to resume river passage on another boat headed for Cincinnati, Memphis, or New Orleans. The jagged rocks in the middle of the river produced a shoal and a shelter for mussels (corrupted to "Muscle Shoals"), their shells a cash crop for the button industry. Donald Davidson, a southern intellectual, wrote in the 1940s of the origins of Muscle Shoals:

> The times [1819] were boisterous, and the settlement of the Great Bend [in the Tennessee River] was like a frolicsome picnic…. At the foot of Muscle Shoals…General John Coffee and his associates of the Cypress Land Company raised up a city. They employed an Italian engineer, Ferdinand Sannoner, to lay out a sumptuous plan of streets and parks upon the uncleared wilderness. Sannoner performed so well that [he was invited] to name the dream city, and he called it Florence after his native home….
>
> Certain great men gave impetus to the speculation [that followed]. General Andrew Jackson and his friends, especially John Coffee, got well acquainted with these lands when they crossed and recrossed the Tennessee during the Creek and Seminole wars. During his expedition to Florida, Jackson camped on York's Bluff [1813], and tradition says that Old Hickory then and there dreamed of a metropolis which would

some day rise at the foot of Muscle Shoals. He put money into his dream...[and] in an incredibly short time, the wilderness of the Great Bend became a genially civilized region where, after the traditional southern pattern, the plantation, the farm, and the frontier merged to produce a life that was neither too rough nor too pretentiously elegant. North Alabama did not quite belong to the Deep South.

Andrew Jackson and his business partners, James Jackson and John Coffee, along with many other prominent people bought land at Muscle Shoals, finding the citizens ambitious and the location comfortable, a soft landscape against a great river, linked by steamboat to the world, and by coach and carriage along the Trace to Nashville and Natchez. John Coffee wrote to Andrew Jackson in 1816 that he decided to settle there because it was "a selected place" presenting a "union of commercial and agricultural advantages." In 1824 Secretary of War John C. Calhoun declared that the solution to navigation at Muscle Shoals was a matter of national interest; and the years of congressional appropriations for a navigable canal at Muscle Shoals began. In 1827 Congress directed the sale of 400,000 acres of national lands, with the proceeds going to Alabama for the purpose of building the canal, which was completed in 1911, eighty-four years later, just as river transport was waning. In 1903 a proposal reached Congress from a group of businessmen who wished to lease rights from the federal government for the construction of a dam and power plant at Muscle Shoals, and business interests bribed and wheedled various senators and congressmen to grant them a franchise. The Progressives believed that public resources should be kept from exploitation by private interests, and the bill provided an opportunity for Roosevelt to make a stand. Gifford Pinchot, Roosevelt's natural resources adviser, prepared a veto message, which the president signed on March 3, 1903. Roosevelt stated, "It does not seem right or just that this element of local value should be given away to private individuals....”

On June 2, 1916, with America at the threshold of war and Progressive Democrat Woodrow Wilson in the White House, a majority in Congress was summoned to fund the Muscle Shoals project. The dam was more than a great engineering feat; it was a monument to political accommodation on Wilson's part. For internationalists like Wilson, the dam was vital to the war effort. The hydroelectric power it generated would be

When it was completed Wilson Dam was the largest masonry structure in the world, a monumental neoclassical public work that later became the centerpiece of a daring concept of decentralization, proposed to Congress by Henry Ford and Thomas Edison in 1921.

used to manufacture nitrates, a necessary ingredient of gunpowder. Nitrates had been imported from Chile to U.S. munitions factories and for export to the Allies until German U-boats blockaded the harbor at Santiago, making it difficult to maintain a supply line. To the Populist isolationists within his own party—particularly William Jennings Bryan, who resigned as Wilson's secretary of state rather than support his foreign policy—the dam with its power stations and nitrate plants, once converted to peacetime use, would be a salvation for the region's farmers, bringing cheap fertilizer, rural electrification, flood control, and other benefits to a poor and isolated region. Mechanics and laborers streamed into Florence in early 1918, first living in a tent village near the dam site on the river. In the years before Ford and Edison came to visit, Florence and Sheffield became boom towns, with a big new payroll for 1,000 federal workers, the largest public works project in the history of the U.S. government up to that time.

It was no accident that the federal government had taken an interest in Muscle Shoals. From its earliest beginnings, it had enjoyed the reputation of a place of progress, a site on the river with a salubrious climate for business and family life. As early as 1812 Tennesseeans who traveled through the region became interested and wrote about schemes to dig a canal linking the Tennessee and the Tombigbee rivers for the improvement of commerce to the Gulf of Mexico. By 1821 regular riverboat service connected Florence, New Orleans, and points between, providing the only commercial transport in and out of the Tennessee Valley until 1830, when the Tuscumbia Railroad Company was founded, the first railroad in the United States west of the Allegheny Mountains.

Beyond its improvements to encourage development, Muscle Shoals was politically progressive, with the

Tennessee Valley (including Lauderdale and Colbert counties) carrying five of only eleven southern counties that supported northern Democrat Stephen Douglas ("In Union there is Strength") against Dixie sympathizer John Breckinridge in 1860. After the vote, the legislators from Muscle Shoals voted against secession. Indeed, an 1855 ordinance granting blacks the right to attend all white schools in Florence was implemented without incident in an era when most southern places had laws banning the teaching of reading, writing, and arithmetic to slaves. Other evidence suggests a progressive, outward-looking spirit. On December 6, 1865, a *Florence Journal* editorial proclaimed, "The old order of things has passed irrevocably away. Landlord and tenant must take the place of master and servant." Two decades later, the same newspaper, remarking on the practice in other parts of Alabama of excluding blacks from voting, reminded its readers, "The fact is there are some men in Alabama who are not yet informed that the Negro in this country is a free man."

On December 3, 1921, Ford and Edison and their wives arrived in Florence on Ford's private railroad car, the *Fair Lane*, making an overnight trip from Detroit. The trip was for publicity. Ford had already quietly toured the Muscle Shoals project the previous June and in July had submitted an offer to the federal government to take over and operate Wilson Dam, the power stations, and the nitrate plants. Ford and Edison, in bowlers and heavy overcoats, posed for photographers before each made brief remarks to a crowd of 3,000, then made a tour of the dam and other facilities. For two days, the locals rubbed shoulders with the celebrities, showing off their southern hospitality with a round of receptions and dinners.

Within a month, Ford had developed a comprehensive proposal that promised to make Florence and the whole Muscle Shoals area the center of a great "75 Mile City," according to the January 12, 1922, *New York*

Times, "[a] plan [that] contemplates one of the greatest undertakings in the history of industrial America...."
Ford's 75 Mile City was made up of a string of large towns and small cities along the Tennessee River. The plan envisioned small factories scattered among residential areas along the banks of the river and up its tributary sloughs and streams, from a point five miles upriver from Florence to seventy miles downstream, where a smaller dam would be built. Workers in the factory would be given leave in the summertime to till a few acres of land at their homesteads so that they could grow their own food and other crops for sale. The factories would run on the vast, cheap power generated by the dam, and the farmer-workers would fertilize their crops from the chemicals produced by the nitrate plant. The power would bring electric lights to the houses and help run the machinery on these small farms.

Ford's proposal was widely publicized. Long articles appeared in the major newspapers, usually on the front page, as the story unfolded in the *Chicago Tribune*, the *Madison Capital Times*, and the *Los Angeles Times* throughout the spring of 1922. At that time Wright was traveling between Spring Green,

Henry Ford and Thomas Edison arrived in Florence on December 3, 1921, to a cheering throng of several hundred citizens. Because he was the best-known figure in America at the time and a rumored candidate for president, Ford's plans for Muscle Shoals became a cause célèbre in Washington and headline news across the country.

Chicago, and the West Coast, busy with house commissions in southern California, where he, like Ford, was also exploring the idea of decentralization and the impact of automobility.

In the September 1922 issue of *Scientific American* Littell McClung reported on Ford's ideas in detail, his account based on Ford's press statements and reports of experiments that Ford had already put in place in the countryside around Detroit. The problem in America, according to McClung and Ford, was that the system of city factories provided a backward, inefficient, and undesirable set of circumstances for factory workers. McClung cited a theoretical example: Bill Jones, a machine worker, purchases 40 acres from Ford at $50 per acre—with a Ford-financed mortgage—two miles from his job. When it is time to plant, Bill is given two weeks off. A professional farm agent, paid by Ford, comes to advise Bill on modern farming methods. Tractors, plows, and other implements are rented for four or five days at a time from the factory to prepare the soil and plant. When Bill and other worker-farmers are not using the machinery, the factory uses it to clear more land for more workers, to transport material, and for other tasks. When the wheat is ready to cut, Bill again takes time off and rents a binder and tractor, again assisted by the farm agent. A community thresher comes along to harvest the crop, which is transported to the cooperative elevator, for which Bill is paid a fair price. The co-op grinds the wheat in an electric mill, then ships out the flour on the waterway.

While Bill is busy assembling cars or making aluminum at the factory, his wife is tending blackberry vines, an apple and pear orchard, and a vegetable garden, with a home demonstrator to show her how to can and make preserves. The Joneses also keep a few chickens and a cow. The surplus milk and eggs are carried to the factory market—Bill drives his Model T or takes a motorboat to work—where he sells to other workers and buys other staples. A healthy part of his factory wage and the proceeds from his crop remain in savings. The Joneses do not have to buy wood or coal for fuel, because their house is heated by cheap electricity, produced at the dam's turbines. Most of their food comes from the land, except for meat, which they buy from a fellow worker who keeps cattle and hunts game, and sells without middlemen at the factory market. All systems are small and self-contained. Schools, shopping, entertainment, churches, and recreational areas are nearby. Jones has a pension, with contributions made by the factory, so that he can retire early, buy more land, and devote full time to farming. His grown sons help out part time while they, too, work at the factory. Agricultural marketing, worker and management training, animal husbandry, and other practical skills are taught in trade schools like those already established by Ford at Highland Park in the Detroit area (as well as by International Harvester and others), which also provide home economics instruction for women, including garment making, food preservation and cooking, and instruction in crafts for use in the home or as money makers.

Along the valley, the factories make alloyed metals, to be fabricated into vehicles at nearby plants or shipped as raw materials to other places. They are fed by a network of mines, all within 100 miles—iron ore from Red Mountain in Birmingham, Arkansas bauxite, Tennessee phosphate. Other factories produce nitrate fertilizer for farmers in the Tennessee Valley or for export across America and throughout the world. Along the river, barges dock at the factories to receive the goods, then lock through the dams, carrying their freight to the Mississippi River and down to the Gulf of Mexico. Transportation along 75 Mile City divides major interstate thoroughfares from farm-to-market and farm-to-factory networks of roads and river lanes for transport of goods by barge, rail, or truck. The entire work force—farmers, factory workers, miners, and transport workers—shares in the benefits of cheap power. Doctors, shopkeepers, and other service providers prosper, reflecting the general standard of living.

McClung's explanation of Ford's vision was based in part on projects such as Ford Homes, a development of 150 ample houses that had been built for workers at Ford's tractor plant in Dearborn. To achieve affordability for his workers, the construction was standardized, although five different models were offered. Pipes for plumbing and heating systems were precut in a factory, and every possible efficiency was employed, including the moving of materials from factory to site along a narrow-gauge railway built down the alleys behind the houses. The financing was also innovative and eliminated speculation, since the developer (Ford) limited his profit to 10 percent and houses, once purchased, could not be resold by the purchaser for seven years.

At first, support for the Ford plan for Muscle Shoals poured into Congress. In a letter to Representative Martin Madden, chairman of the committee considering Ford's proposal, R. R. Moton, principal of Alabama's Tuskegee Institute, observed that "the plight of the Negro farmer and farm worker in the South could not be much worse than it is," and suggested that the "offer contains the hope of improving the fortunes of millions of people.... It is the duty of Congress to give Mr. Ford the chance to make good on his offer." Ford presented 75 Mile City as a model project, declaring in a press release that "neither he nor any of his heirs [would] realize any monetary benefit from the Muscle Shoals plants or the power developed...[making] the project, if the Government gives its consent, the outstanding achievement of his career."

By the next year, as Ford was negotiating to lease the dam and nitrate plants at Muscle Shoals and publicizing his ideas, others were cashing in on the newfound celebrity of Muscle Shoals. The Howell & Graves real estate company in New York bought several hundred acres of land and set up the Muscle Shoals Intelligence Bureau, a boiler room operation to sell twenty-foot lots to small investors across the country:

> Would you, if you could, associate yourself with the world's greatest manufacturer and industrial genius—HENRY FORD?
>
> [T]housands of people have become independently wealthy through the development of Ford's gigantic industrial plants in Detroit, Michigan. Mr. Ford has recently stated that he would employ one million men and build a city seventy-five miles long at MUSCLE SHOALS where the government has already spent $117,000,000 in industrial plants, etc.
>
> You have not had the opportunity to affiliate yourself with Mr. Ford's successes of the past, but you may profit and prosper by his operations of the future if you are in a position to.

The Ford people made complaints to the Better Business Bureau, but the speculation, which was widely promoted, contributed to killing the Muscle Shoals project in Washington. More important, the bill to lease the Muscle Shoals district to Henry Ford was whipsawed by two opposing but influential constituencies. On one side, a powerful private utilities lobby, led by the Alabama Power Company in Birmingham, made an all-out effort to kill the Ford proposal, which would have completely undercut the company's rate base. On the other side, Progressives, led by Republican Senator George W. Norris from Nebraska and Robert La Follette from Wisconsin, fought any privatization of natural resources. Norris pointed to the example of a hydroelectric power station on the Saint Lawrence River. Electricity on the American side of the river, where the power was privately controlled, sold at five to six times the rate on the Canadian side, where it was owned publicly. Whatever promises Ford made regarding profits, Norris did not trust them. Influential in the fight was another Pro-

The Howell & Graves storefront real estate office, located only two blocks from Ford Motor Company's New York headquarters, featured a large mural of Muscle Shoals, with highlights of the new developments. The 25-foot-long painting is accurate in its details, including the Howell & Graves school, which still stands on Wilson Dam Highway across from Euclid Avenue in what is now Muscle Shoals City. The tree-lined road that was to serve as a main street is now being planned—75 years later—as a new gateway to the region.

gressive, Gifford Pinchot, who as Theodore Roosevelt's adviser two decades earlier had opposed private control of Muscle Shoals.

Increasingly, a split developed between the Progressives and the conservatives, led by Wilson's successor as president, Warren Harding. Harding died in 1923, in his third year in office. His successor, Calvin Coolidge, received an early pledge of support from Ford, who had been entertaining a run for the presidency, and in return supported the Muscle Shoals proposal, an effort that was apparently halfhearted. Ford was indeed a substantial threat to Coolidge as probably the most famous and admired man in America at the time. Secretary of War John Wingate Weeks had made the first approach to Ford about leasing Muscle Shoals, and it was Weeks whom Ford blamed for the rejection by Congress. "Ford felt [Weeks was] probably influenced by the utilities group, " remembered E. G. Liebold. While the Ford offer was great publicity for all concerned, political and financial problems were impossible to overcome.

The defeat of the Muscle Shoals plan was devastating to the people of the area, whose hopes were with Henry Ford. Bit by bit, the federal government completed the Wilson Dam, but the local population saw little of the promised prosperity. Across the dam, east of Sheffield, streets with sidewalks—Dearborn Avenue, Michigan Street, Highland Park Drive—had been laid out by Howell & Graves in what was to be Ford City. Now the streets disappeared into cotton fields, the sidewalks, under brambles.

3. THE REGIONALISTS

Wright's mother, Anna, died at 83 in 1923 and his mentor, Louis Sullivan, in 1924. He lost his first home in Oak Park when he left in 1910, and Taliesin I, which was destroyed by fire. Thirteen years after separating from his first wife, Catherine, Frank Lloyd Wright obtained a divorce, and a year after that—November 12, 1923—belatedly married Christian Scientist and Tennessean Miriam Noel in a midnight wedding ceremony on a bridge over the Wisconsin River. Five months later they separated. Miriam moved to Chicago, then Los Angeles; Wright stayed at Taliesin. He was depressed, alone, and deeply in debt. The country had become politically more conservative, socially more frivolous. Wright called the era "kaleidoscopic," its "social-shifts demanded and taken by the ruthless to and fro of our artificial, hectic, economic life in the

United States." Washington was rocked by the Teapot Dome scandals. Robert La Follette of Wisconsin, who, like Wright, Jenkin Lloyd-Jones, and Henry Ford, had opposed Wilson's war policies, died in 1925 after an unsuccessful third-party campaign for the presidency on the Progressive ticket in 1924.

Wright's work in the early 1920s was mostly in California. These commissions began after his work on the

Both daring and originality helped Wright secure commissions from Edward H. Doheny and other West Coast tycoons. The Doheny Ranch (1921) project in the Sierra Madre Mountains provided the ultimate integration of site and structures.

Imperial Hotel in Tokyo, when he met heiress Aline Barnsdall and designed an expensive, fortress-like compound for her at Olive Hill in Los Angeles. Other California fantasy projects with elaborate site plans followed: an "Emerald City" in 1921 for financier Edward H. Doheny, a ranch high in the Sierra Madre Mountains, which was dashed by Doheny's involvement in the Teapot Dome scandal; an earlier project for A. M. Johnson, a desert retreat and religious shrine at Death Valley in 1922; and a resort at Lake Tahoe with floating cabins, also designed in 1922, another victim of Teapot Dome. His California projects also included his textile-block houses, an experiment with concrete block as a building material for inexpensive housing, the forerunner of construction for the Usonian house, but practically demonstrated first in residential projects for wealthy clients. His son Lloyd supervised these projects, which included the Millard (1923), Storer (1923), Ennis (1924), and Freeman (1924) houses. All used patterned concrete block in their construction, employing a single system for inside and out.

In California Wright issued a 1923 manifesto against the city in the wake of death and destruction on the other side of the Pacific Rim, a devastating earthquake that struck downtown Tokyo. *Experimenting with Human Lives* was a treatise against the skyscraper ("Yankee expedients [that are] poison to Tokio culture") and his first declaration of war on the city. "Naturally restricted areas [were] temporarily relieved by invention of the skyscraper—before [the] advent of electrical transmission and the automobile," declared Wright, showing his deference to Louis Sullivan, who was then still alive. Wright proposed a restriction on the height of buildings to three to five stories, forcing "funerals among ground-speculators.... Modern transportation may scatter the city, open breathing spaces in it, green it and beautify it, making it fit for a superior order of human beings."

65

In 1924 Wright met and fell in love with Olgivanna Hinzenberg, a woman in her mid-twenties who had been born in Montenegro and had lived most recently in France. She had been married to a Russian architect and had a daughter but was by then separated. So Wright began life again at age 58, spending weekends at the Congress Hotel in Chicago, working on a glass and copper skyscraper for A. M. Johnson of the National Life Insurance Company. With Olgivanna's arrival Miriam began a relentless campaign of vituperative assaults, warrants, lawsuits, and restraining orders to destroy his life and practice. When Wright was joined by Olgivanna and her daughter Svetlana at Spring Green in February 1925, matters moved from bad to worse. They suffered another terrible fire at Taliesin that spring, then escaped to Puerto Rico in early 1926 to avoid unfavorable press attention generated by Miriam's charges.

Olgivanna Wright, c. 1932

With little or no work, an outcast from polite society, Wright first turned to the rebuilding of Taliesin, borrowing funds from the Bank of Wisconsin and using the house and its contents as collateral. He also turned to writing, producing a nine-part series of technical articles that appeared in *Architectural Record* from May 1927 through December 1928 and paid him $7,500. Unable to meet his monthly obligations, he went to New York over the 1926–27 holidays to oversee the forced auction sale of 346 Japanese prints at the Anderson Galleries at 59th Street and Park Avenue, raising only $35,000 of an appraised value of over $100,000. By the first thaw, the bank sold all of the livestock at Taliesin and prepared to complete foreclosure on the house and buildings. In May, Miriam sued Wright for his failure to make alimony payments. On top of everything else Olgivanna was threatened with deportation.

A string of lawyers were hired, then often ignored. Philip La Follette, younger son of Robert La Follette and an aspiring politician, took on the job, deflecting creditors, the bank, and the "outraged wife" and her lawyers as best he could, following advice given by Chicago lawyer Clarence Darrow. ("Your case is not a legal one, Frank. What you need is the advice of some wise man of the world who will be your friend and who will see you through.") A group of Wright's friends was eventually assembled to bail him out. In August 1927, Frank Lloyd Wright, Inc., began to circulate a prospectus to raise $75,000 to satisfy the bank's interest in Taliesin and pay other immediate debts, placing the Wrights on a strict household allowance. It required nearly a year to capitalize. Wright declared that they were incorporating "what looked like a lost cause," even as a dozen friends, former clients, and family members subscribed. Wright finally was granted a divorce; the bank evicted him and Olgivanna from Taliesin; the new "stockholders" negotiated a settlement with creditors; architect Albert MacArthur, son of Charles MacArthur (of the Biltmore Hotels), hired Wright to rework the Arizona Biltmore in Scottsdale; Wright, Olgivanna, and Svetlana traveled to Arizona, then established a household in a beach cottage at the Valencia in La Jolla, California; Miriam found them, trashed the cottage, and swore out a warrant for "immorality on the part of her husband."

Wright craved a hearth and home, a return to productive work, a chance for a new beginning. Disciplined, practical Olgivanna led the way through this dark passage of bankruptcy and disgrace, which included two nights in jail, then through a slow, fitful, uncertain, erratic, eccentric climb out of the depths into a new life with a refreshed vision, a new family, friends, clients, students, and colleagues at his side. Almost as an afterthought, Frank Lloyd Wright and Olgivanna, christened Olga Ivanovna Milan Lazovich, were married August 25, 1928, at Rancho Santa Fe, a resort in La Jolla, California.

Publicity about Wright's private life took its toll on his career. By the late 1920s he had few commissions, and writing became increasingly important to his work. Olgivanna urged him to write his autobiography. In some respects Louis Sullivan's *Autobiography of an Idea*, published in 1924, was his model, but Wright wrote in the first person where Sullivan's self-portrait employed the impersonal third. Wright's manuscript was published in 1932 by Longmans, Green of New York. Despite substantial editing it was, and is, difficult for the reader, in part because of its stream-of-consciousness prose, a journey both enlightening and confusing.

The result of these years for Wright was an even greater alienation from established norms. The America he would envision was an America without lawyers or bankers, middle-class prudishness, or bourgeois taste. For him, the idea of rent and landlords, indeed, the absentee ownership of land, ran counter to the democratic spirit. Two pieces that preceded his autobiography, entitled "In Bondage" and "The Usonian City," used the city as a metaphor for his marital problems. "The Usonian City," incorporating an amalgamation of progressive ideas that emerged after World War I, was Wright's response to an evolving social science consensus: the city as it existed was no longer the complete answer for the future of American civilization. Others shared his vision of an America without cities. Traffic, dirt, corruption, and overcrowded tenements provoked a movement in the progressive press for reform and stimulated discussion at Hull House, in the pages of *The Nation* and *The New Republic*, and even among architects. The 1920s were the time of Wright's first substantial encounter with the eastern intellectual establishment, specifically with architectural critic Lewis Mumford and his milieu. Wright first sought out Mumford, inviting him to lunch at the Plaza Hotel in January 1927, when Wright was in New York for the disposal of his Japanese print collection. Mumford had contributed a piece entitled "The Social Back Ground of Frank Lloyd Wright" to "The Life of the American Architect Frank Lloyd Wright," a series that had appeared in seven issues of the Dutch architecture magazine *Wendingen* in 1925. At about the same time Wright read Mumford's *Sticks and Stones*, including his ideas of how civilization followed architecture through the ages. The scope of Mumford's ideas was exciting to Wright, and he recognized a kindred spirit and an intellect receptive to his own ideas. Many years later Wright wrote to Mumford, "[*Sticks and Stones*] was prophetic at a crucial time," a call for salvation from the conformity of historic ornament and conventional form. Mumford, a full generation younger than Wright, discovered Wright's work in the context of his own first explorations into regional planning and modern architecture. To him, Wright's architecture served to define an American culture. Wright was awed by Mumford's erudition: "If I could write like you," wrote Wright to Mumford in 1931, "I might put the cause of Modern Architecture over single-handed."

Mumford's mentor had been Patrick Geddes of Edinburgh, the first pioneer of regional planning, whose "Valley Plan for Civilization" replaced maps and the physical arrangement of development with concepts to benefit the health and welfare of a population. (Geddes was perhaps the first observer to consider electricity as "a magic wand" that would emancipate women.) Like Wright, Mumford was an admirer of Henry Ford. In *Sticks and Stones* he had called Ford "a technological genius...[who has] been quick to see the possibilities of little factories set in the midst of the countryside." Neither was ever affiliated with any political party or organization, yet both sought influence in political realms. Mumford's politics were collectivist, Wright's individualistic. Mumford's interest was in housing, Wright's interest was in houses. But they shared an understanding of architecture as a spirit that wraps all of the culture of a time into a package: in the words of the epigraph Mumford chose for *Sticks and Stones*, "as civilization itself."

During the 1920s Wright and Mumford followed parallel paths. Mumford was a founding member of the regional planning movement in the United States and the Regional Planning Association of America. As Carl Sussman's history has documented, many of the charter members of the RPAA learned their skills in service to the federal government during the war years: Henry Wright and Frederick Lee Ackerman worked for the Emergency Fleet Corporation, one of the groups to build the first public housing in the United States; Benton MacKaye worked for the Department of Labor beginning in 1918–19 on an innovative plan that has been described by Roy Lubove as no less than "a national program of community-building whose corollary benefits included preservation and efficient utilization of the national domain, full employment, and the complete reorganization of the farming, lumbering, and mining industries." Stuart Chase was engaged in economic planning for the War Industries Board; Mumford was in the navy. The group first formed in Washington during the war, when Charles Whitaker, editor of the *Journal of the American Institute of Architects*, used his position to promote government housing for veterans, recruiting Ackerman, Henry Wright, architect Clarence Stein, and MacKaye into his circle. In 1919 he helped to organize an AIA committee on community planning, which was later chaired by Stein and Henry Wright and published reports drafted by Mumford.

The planning movement was interdisciplinary. Thorstein Veblen at Chicago laid out a program for a planned economy, while social philosopher John Dewey and *The New Republic* founding editor Herbert Croly promoted projects and ideas that involved the government in development, with historian Charles Beard providing a historical context for planning. An urgent need for low-cost housing for returning veterans led to initiatives around the country. Jane Addams of Hull House became chair of the Public Housing Association in Illinois.

All of these developments had been percolating for a very long time. Beginning in the second third of the 19th century, the romantic impulse to groom the countryside had introduced the idea of landscape planning into educated circles. The foundations had been put in place by Thomas Jefferson and Ralph Waldo Emerson: individualism, a love of nature, and an overwhelming sense that America s destiny was in its vast, open spaces. Translating words to pictures, Andrew Jackson Downing (1815–52) promoted landscape architecture as a civilizing influence:

> So long as men are forced to dwell in log huts and follow the hunter's life, we must not be surprised at lynch laws and the use of the bowie knife. But when smiling lawns and tasteful cottages begin to embellish a country, we know that order and culture are established..

He was joined in this mission by Alexander Jackson Davis (1803–92) and followed by nurseryman-turned-park planner Frederick Law Olmsted (1822–1903) and by writers such as Henry David Thoreau (1817–62) and Walt Whitman (1819–92).

The movement also drew on a utopian strain in the work of Englishmen—Henry George, Ebenezer Howard, Peter Kropotkin (actually a Romanoff prince in exile), and Raymond Unwin, all of whom were influenced by earlier utopian writers like Thomas Spence and Samuel Butler. George's *Progress and Poverty* proposed to remove land from private ownership so that society as a whole, rather than a few landlords, would benefit from rising land values. In his *Fields, Factories and Workshops*, published in the 1890s, Kropotkin, a visionary anarchist, imagined electrical and communications grids, express highways and high speed automobiles, motion pictures and television as humanistic uses of technology to transform the world, merging city and country life. Ebenezer Howard, who had first seen an extensive parks system in Chicago, when he lived there, developed the idea of garden cities that had a predefined boundary and density, surrounded by a natural buffer to protect the countryside from urban encroachments. Howard himself was influenced by the communitarian ideas of industrialist Robert Owen, another English utopian. Finally, it was the architect Raymond Unwin, a disciple of William Morris's Arts and Crafts movement in England, who led the town planning movement into the 1920s and actually designed and built the first garden city, Letchworth, with his partner Barry Parker, providing precedent for the New York metropolitan planner Thomas Adams, who was the leading practitioner of conventional regional planning on the garden city model in the United States (and creator of the New York Port Authority). By the 1920s, planning for patterns of development had evolved to include whole regions as an organizing framework, with and without architectural harmony, but incorporating new developments in transportation and communications built on theories of political economy and social progress.

The RPAA held its first meeting in 1923 and soon was meeting frequently with an unwieldy agenda, advanced by informal consensus. Works such as H. G. Wells's *Anticipations of the Reaction of Mechanical and Scientific Progress upon Human Life and Thought*, Edward Bellamy's *Looking Backward*, Kropotkin's book, and, later, Fritz Lang's film *Metropolis* all informed the discussion and helped to prepare this earnest band for the future, with each technological breakthrough another step forward. In 1925 the RPAA raised its collective voice in a series of articles published in *Survey Graphic*. Perhaps the most important of these was a piece by Mumford, "The Fourth Migration." According to Mumford, America's first migration, the movement of settlement across the Alleghenies, sought land; the second sought manufacturing centers in industrial towns and along railroads; and the third sought the financial centers of great cities, creating a civilization based on currency exchange. A fourth migration was required to consolidate the other three, a migration based on the technological revolution that began in 1900 and was roaring like a speedboat through the 20th century. From his 1925 vantage point, Mumford explained that in the earlier migrations, the telegraph symbolically followed the railroad, with people, materials, and communications moving down the line in a single point-to-point series of interconnections. With the automobile, telephone exchanges, parcel post and rural mail delivery, hydroelectric power, and, later, radio, the line became a network, a vast web of agencies of decentralization. Mumford also saw in vague outline what later became television, satellite communications, and air shuttles: "The fourth migration is only beginning: we may either permit it to crystallize in a formation quite as bad as those of our earlier migrations, or we may turn it to better account by leading it into new channels."

All through his professional life Frank Lloyd Wright's interactions with the academic, government, and political communities were fleeting yet frequent. With acquaintances and friends such as historians Ferdinand Schevill and Charles Beard at the University of Chicago and Alexander Meikeljohn at the University of Wisconsin, in addition to Mumford, Clarence Stein, Jens Jensen, and others, Wright certainly had personal contact with regional planners and their followers by the late 1920s. He was also an avid reader, absorbing their rationale for decentralization as quickly as their ideas reached print in the architectural journals and progressive magazines to which he subscribed. To an extraordinary degree, Wright was able to appropriate these ideas and expand their meaning, finding architectural content in the most abstract concepts. He had few commissions during most of the 1920s, but toward the end of the decade a client provided him with the opportunity to combine theory and practice.

Frank Lloyd Wright's grand landscape projects of the 1920s culminated in the design of a resort hotel in the Arizona desert commissioned by Alexander Chandler for Californians made rich by movies and petroleum. All of these western projects were canceled when the stock market crashed in 1929.

In January 1929 Wright received a commission from a wealthy hotel owner, Alexander Chandler, to design a winter resort hotel in the Arizona desert outside Phoenix. Faced with the problem of housing his assistants and household near the site, Wright designed an encampment, located between San Marcos in the Desert, as the resort was named, and a ranch called Broad-acres. The camp, which he christened Ocotillo (for the cactus; actually, Ocatillo in his version of the spelling), was built of rough lumber and canvas, a compound of working, sleeping, and living spaces around the focal point of a communal campfire where Wright presided, surrounded by his assistants and family. In its ambience, which had more in common with that of a revivalist camp meeting than a design office, and in its organization Ocotillo was most obviously a model for the Taliesin Fellowship, which would be established a few years later. But its importance lay also in its conception as an ensemble of buildings and spaces that served to connect the lives of its occupants with their natural surroundings. Built far from the city, set close to the ground and across the landscape, made of the most minimal materials, Ocotillo was an experiment in the principles of the Usonian house and Broadacre City. The resort itself, however, was never realized. Along with a concurrent project for housing in New York City, St. Marks-in-the-Bouwerie, it was wiped out by the October 1929 stock market crash.

Up until the Wall Street crash, the interplay of people, ideas, and ideals in the era of bathtub gin and sky's-the-limit fantasies imbued Wright with a renewed sense of mission and purpose. Now debt and depression set in. He was in his sixties, and his world was rapidly changing. Recognized by Philip Johnson in 1932 as "the greatest architect of the 19th century," Wright witnessed a boom in construction in America in the late 1920s that almost completely passed him by. His clientele—self-made midwestern men of wealth—disappeared, first because of his scandalous private life, then because of the crash. Wright's new prospective clients, intellectuals who were interested in his ideas, had neither the wherewithal nor the risk-taking spirit to engage him as an architect.

Toward the end of 1929 he received an invitation from Princeton University to give a series of lectures the

Ocotillo was Wright's home and studio in the desert that also served as a model for a camp for construction workers for Alexander Chandler's resort hotel, San Marcos in the Desert, and eventually contributed to the conceptualization of Broadacre City, named for Broad-acres, a ranch next to the camp.

following June, providing a substantial honorarium donated by Otto Hermann Kahn, president and chairman of the board of the Metropolitan Opera Company. "It was," according to Frederick Gutheim, "the turning point in Mr. Wright's career." Wright remarked, "[as a] journeyman preacher...[I] earn[ed] the only fees anywhere in sight at that bad time of my life. This began to look like recognition at home." The Kahn lectures led to other lectures, which led to the idea of Wright as an educator, which led to the Taliesin Fellowship. Lectures also led to more writing, which brought media attention, which would lead to commissions for his signature buildings—Johnson Wax, Fallingwater, the Guggenheim Museum—and to the Usonian house.

Although Wright despised formal education, he loved the attention and adoration of students. (He was not Princeton's first choice. J. J. P. Oud from Holland, a European pioneer of the modern movement, was first approached, but had to decline because of the illness of a family member.) For Princeton Wright laid out a European-style manifesto for the future in six lectures. The fourth, "The Cardboard House," captured the essence of Wright's ideal American house—on which the Usonian house was based—in nine rules of organic architecture. The first rule was the reduction of the number of necessary parts of the house, keeping the number of separate rooms to a minimum, creating a sense of unity among the various parts. Wright also stressed the importance of eliminating walls that create boxlike rooms and of completely eliminating basements, pointing out the need to "harmonize all necessary openings to 'outside' or to 'inside' with good human proportions." The second rule called for associating the building as a whole with its site by emphasizing horizontal planes. He suggested reducing the number of different materials and eliminating ornament that did not relate to the nature of materials. Moving on to the mechanics of a house, he stressed the importance of incorporating all heating, lighting, and plumbing so that "these systems became constituent parts of the building itself." Finally, Wright also called for the incorporation of furnishings, "making them all one with the building and designing them in simple terms for machine work," using "straight lines and rectilinear forms," eliminating the need for a decorator.

The final lecture, "The City," began with a sophistical question: "Is the city a natural triumph of the herd instinct over humanity...or is [it] only a persistent form of social disease[?]..." Throughout the series, Wright characterized the machine as the irresistible, unstoppable juggernaut that moved society into the slavery of urban congestion. The instrument of destruction, according to Wright, could now be used as an instrument of renewal. "The Machine, once our formidable adversary, is ready and competent to undertake the drudgeries of living on this Earth. The margin of leisure even now widens as the Machine succeeds. This margin should be expanded and devoted to making beautiful the environment in which human beings are born to live—into which one brings the children who will be the Usonia of tomorrow."

In the next breath, Wright laid out his concept of individualism and his vision for a new America: "...The Machine...will enable all that was human in the city to go to the country...[to] enable human life to be based fairly and squarely on the ground....It will soon become unnecessary to concentrate in masses for any purpose whatsoever. The individual unit, in more sympathetic grouping on the ground, will grow stronger in the hard earned freedom gained at first by that element of the city not prostitute to the Machine. Henry Ford stated this idea in his plans for the development of Muscle Shoals."

Far away from the city, unlike Chicago's trolley suburbs, the place Wright described was not dependent on anything but the network of roads and wirescape and the web of communication, transportation, and water power that would create bounty where only poverty then existed. Wright's prescription for America included predictions that in these new expanses all of a family's needs would be within an easy distance and that the "movies, 'talkies' and all, would soon be seen and heard better at home than in any hall...[along with] symphony concerts, operas and lectures." He declared, "The home of the individual social unit will contain in itself...all the city heretofore could afford, plus intimate comfort and free individual choice."

Departing from Ford's Muscle Shoals, Wright concluded "The City" by discussing his decentralization ideas in terms of an appropriate architecture, synthesizing two concepts that had so far developed on separate tracks. "Eventually we must live for the Beautiful whether we want to or not. Our industrial champion Henry Ford was forced to recognize this—probably not connecting the beautiful with Art, 'the Bunk.' Just as he did in his industry, so America will be compelled to allow necessity its own honest beauty, or die a death nowise different from the nations whose traditions we accepted and idolized." (Later, in developing the details for Broadacre City, Wright proposed the establishment of a design center as the governing body for his new community, with architects, rather than lawyers, serving as arbiters, legislators, and constabulary.)

A few months after Princeton, when Wright was in Chicago addressing the National Terra Cotta Society, he expanded his tribute to Henry Ford:

> He is a man of common sense. He is a man that really has contributed a great deal to our country. He has successful ideas. His proposition for Muscle Shoals was one of the best things that I have heard of as a solution of the excess machine increment...What to do with man at the machine? Ford's proposal was for the decentralization of industry. If

79

he could get Muscle Shoals he was going to have lots of little factories. He was going to give every man a few acres of ground of his own. In the summer the men would work on the ground. In the winter they would go to work with their machines in the factory, the machines in the factory giving such facility that they need only work at the machines 5 or 6 months of each year.

Ford and Wright shared an engineer's faith that anything could be accomplished through design and organization. Ford said, "the best the past has left us in industry is its designs, [which] have expanded illimitably since the arrival of industry with its extension of service and its encouragement of individual effort." Both men believed that standardization would support both economy and individualism. Ford said, "to my mind it is starting wrong to put methods ahead of purpose," which is in the same spirit as Wright's "form and function are one." Both were obsessed with quality. Both men were all-American, pacifist isolationists. Both had a strain of xenophobia: just as Wright criticized the European socialist architecture of the Bauhaus, Ford imagined a conspiracy among European Jewish bankers and Wall Street. Both were hostile to unions and what they represented, but were impressed by experiments in Soviet Russia, where both men's ideas were influential. Both loved nature. Ford used naturalist John Burroughs as his guide; Wright consulted Thoreau. Both revered Thomas Jefferson.

Ford's Muscle Shoals inspired Wright's Usonia, later refined into Broadacre City. Muscle Shoals indeed became Wright's Erehwon, the place that was nowhere and everywhere, where people's homes, work places, and recreation places all were blended harmoniously with their natural setting. Like Ford's ideas, Mumford's vision for a decentralized America made a great impression on Wright. Together, they helped to elaborate an idea that seemed to contradict the trends of a generation, the move of a rural population to the city for jobs and sophistication, a move that created a new political constituency and an overload of need for housing, social services, transit, and law enforcement. For these visionaries, particularly Ford, the answer to America's urban ills was in the creation of jobs away from cities—the concept for village industries that he tested in Michigan and proposed for Muscle Shoals—that would attract a work force, stimulate economic and cultural development, and engender prosperity across rural landscapes. While Ford's interests were directed to the creation of jobs and wealth through manufacturing and distribution systems, Mumford's emphasis was on infrastructure—roads, electric power, and housing—patterns of development that were respectful of the environment yet accommodated growth. Embracing these concepts, Wright sought to give a form to decentralization, first in a model "city" that was not a city at all, and then in buildings that in themselves articulated the idea of decentralization.

Writing to Mumford soon after the lectures, Wright reported that he was asked at Princeton what he thought of Mumford. "The most valuable critic our country has—a mind of Emersonian quality—with true creative power," was his reply. In Wright's pantheon of greatness for those living in his own time, only Ford the industrialist and Mumford the intellectual stood with himself the architect to support his hope for America.

82

(Opposite) Pickwick Dam, near Muscle Shoals, was an early TVA project. Its designers, led by Austrian Roland Wank, employed sophicated modernism in an effort to create a contemporary American style of architecture.

4. THE TENNESSEE VALLEY AUTHORITY

In early 1931 a manifesto, *I'll Take My Stand*, was published in New York, becoming an overnight cause célèbre in New York and Washington. The book was an anthology, started at the English department at Nashville's Vanderbilt University by Donald Davidson, Allen Tate, Rob Ransom, and others. They were conservatives who called themselves Southern Agrarians, as social reformers, and the Fugitives, as poets. They believed that true art could never be the product of a displaced bohemian life but could be created only by a people rooted in a provincial and conservative society. In 1925, when they were still formulating a catechism, John Scopes went on trial in Dayton, Tennessee. As Paul Conklin wrote in *The Southern Agrarians*, "Regional self-consciousness seemed inescapable in the year of the Scopes Trial," when critics like H. L. Mencken and

Frank Kent were ridiculing Tennesseans in print. Such disparagement of the South had been a popular sport since Reconstruction. All southerners, from Charleston gentry to Appalachian rustics, were the targets of derision. Some saw southerners as rugged individualists, endowed with charm and a sense of history; to many northerners, however, that individualism was most noticeably displayed by xenophobic racists, indolent illiterates, and Bible-thumping reactionaries, all hostile to progress. To many who read about its proposed development in the *New York Times,* a place such as Muscle Shoals was an inaccessible backwater. With *I'll Take My Stand* an instant sensation, the regional planners decided to search for common ground with their southern brethren.

Lewis Brownlow, a former commissioner of Washington, D.C., during the Wilson administration, and the leading light of dozens of organizations and committees, organized a Roundtable on Regionalism for July 1931 at the University of Virginia, bringing together North and South for intensive discussion on regional planning and related topics, following a Mumford adage that "regionalism must be made the cultural motive for regional planning...if it isn't to relapse into arid technological schemes." Henry Wright, who had written most of an ambitious regional plan for the state of New York, and who assisted Brownlow and Clarence Stein with the arrangements for the conference, wrote to Mumford that "the reason regionalism was chosen for the Roundtable, rather than regional planning, was to...[divert attention from]...the more obvious and mechanical expressions of planning, and get down to the fundamentals of a newer and better organization of life and its relation to its natural inheritance, in contrast to the life now developed in the most 'advanced' portions of the country."

The Roundtable, meeting in the South, outside the "advanced" portion of the country, was important in that it was probably the first time New York and Washington liberal intellectuals like Stein, Mumford, Frederick Gutheim, and Henry Wright were exposed to the brand of regionalism espoused at Nashville, Chapel Hill, and Charlottesville. From the South, the leading figure at the conference was the Arkansan poet John Gould Fletcher. The featured speaker was New York Governor Franklin Roosevelt, who was already a candidate for president. "He told us about his notion of river development" and provided, according to Brownlow, what amounted to a "complete blueprint of the yet-to-come Tennessee Valley Authority and the Columbia Valley development; but not one of the entire audience seemed to sense the significance of what he was saying."

One person who did understand both the significance of Roosevelt's speech and the future possibilities of regional planning was Frederick Gutheim. A few years earlier he had been a student at the Experimental College at the University of Wisconsin and had studied under Mumford, among others, and edited the *Wisconsin Literary Magazine*, following in the footsteps of Frederick Jackson Turner, its former editor. He was inspired by his work under faculty member John Gaus on a study of creative forces in America after the Civil War and by Gaus's work as chairman of the governor's planning committee. He began to spend weekends at Taliesin and befriended Wright's unpaid assistant Henry Klumb. Gutheim, who had a car, treated Klumb to weekend excursions. He also drove Philip La Follette, Wright's lawyer and the organizer of Frank Lloyd Wright, Inc., to political meetings as La Follette prepared to run for governor.

"The potato-and-cabbage odor of rural poverty hung over the Wright household,...with the only heat coming from the hearth," remembered Gutheim. Feeling guilty about being a guest and eating at Taliesin every weekend, Gutheim began to organize, index, and classify Wright's papers. "It was an enormous job, a huge project," said Gutheim. "Everything was in a mess." The image of self-imposed isolation that Wright cultivated "was a myth," according to Gutheim. "He took all the relevant magazines at the time, maintained an enormous correspondence, and constantly traveled."

By the time of the Charlottesville conference, Gutheim had left Wisconsin, moved to Washington, and found a job at the Brookings Institution. While a follower of Stein and Mumford, he did not think that they knew much about politics. "They were not sophisticated about the ways of Washington," he said later. By the next year he was working on a legislative initiative that would turn Roosevelt's generalities and George Norris's ideas for public power at Muscle Shoals into a more ambitious regional plan for the Tennessee Valley. At the Brookings Institution, during Roosevelt's first hundred days in office, Gutheim wrote Sections 22 and 23 of the Tennessee Valley Authority Act of 1933, the single most important piece of social legislative of that session of Congress, a landmark statute in the cause of regional planning. He went on to work with Catherine Bauer at the U.S. Housing Authority during Roosevelt's second term as the information director (Bauer headed the division for research and information). He would later edit a book of Wright's essays, speeches, and articles, work on the Committee on Theme at the New York World's Fair, become the first architecture critic for a daily U. S. newspaper, found the historic preservation program at George Washington University, and author the definitive history of the Potomac River.

After Princeton, Wright went on the lecture circuit, speaking at the New School for Social Research in New York, and in Seattle, Denver, Philadelphia, Madison, Minneapolis, Milwaukee, and Chicago (at the Art

Institute and at a convention of the National Terra Cotta Society). In 1931, with the help of the two temporary stenographers he had hired to help him complete his autobiography, he took the message of his Princeton lectures to a wider public. An article, "Broadacre City: An Architect's Vision," appeared in the *New York Times Magazine* in March 1932, and a book, *The Disappearing City*, was also published that year. They would be the first of many iterations of his Usonian vision.

The mood in the country was desperate. On March 7, outside Henry Ford's River Rouge factory, 3,000 unemployed workers who marched in zero degree weather were greeted with tear gas when they did not disperse; when they threw rocks and frozen mud, the authorities responded, drenching the marchers with freezing water from fire hoses, then firing their revolvers and even machine guns, the hail of bullets killing four and injuring dozens. In the midst of national turmoil and despair, Wright introduced his cure for the ills of the city, a blast against centralization, skyscrapers, and speculators. In the *New York Times* article he declared, "Broadacre City is not merely the only democratic city. It is the only possible city, looking forward to the future." He characterized the offices and apartments of urban life as "the shelf and the pigeon hole...[offered as] landlord expedients." Wright's article was timed in part to counter what he considered an insulting juxtaposition of his work with the upstart Europeans in the Museum of Modern Art's "Modern Architecture: International Exhibition." With Roosevelt the leading candidate for the Democratic Party's presidential nomination, Wright's unveiling of Broadacre City was also the opening of his own campaign to transform the American landscape. He wrote Mumford in January, "I consented to join the affair thinking I would be among peers: I heard only of Corbusier, Mies et al. I found a handpicked select group including [Raymond]

Hood and Neutra...." Wright was furious that he had been included in a show with Neutra, a former assistant of his whom he charged with a variety of misdemeanors.

Whether Roosevelt took notice of Wright's ideas at this time is a matter of speculation. In 1931 Wright had had a copy of his Princeton lectures sent to the then governor of New York. Roosevelt may have seen the news coverage of the International Style exhibition, which had been running in New York since early February. If he noticed the exhibition, however, it was probably not because of a passionate interest in modern architecture or in Wright, but because of his commitment to planning and housing. Lewis Mumford had written a long piece on public housing for the catalog (with assistance from Catherine Bauer), criticizing President Hoover's Conference on Home Building.

During his campaign for the Democratic nomination for president, Roosevelt returned again and again to the urgent need for national planning, including an impassioned speech on regional planning that he delivered over national radio in early April 1932. It took 75 days between Roosevelt's inauguration, on March 4, 1933, and Thursday, May 18, for him to sign the Tennessee Valley Authority Act. At the White House, Frederic Delano and aide Rexford Tugwell coordinated the legislation with Senator Norris on Capitol Hill. Norris's last Muscle Shoals bill had passed Congress in 1931, only to be vetoed by President Hoover. Frederick Gutheim asked John Nolen, Jr., and Charles Eliot II (another landscape architect and a former partner in the firm founded by Frederick Law Olmsted) at the National Capital Parks and Planning Commission to help promote the TVA bill to Delano, who had also served as chairman of the commission. Together they went to Norris, who had been interested in TVA only as a power-generating agency organized on a Canadian

The generator room at Wilson Dam, Muscle Shoals, before TVA, c. 1930. TVA was first conceived as a project only for Muscle Shoals. Designated as the TVA headquarters, the area almost immediately became an outpost as public officials sought the conveniences of Knoxville, Tennessee, which was more populous and closer to the power centers in Washington and to construction sites for the largest of the new dams.

model. Gutheim remembered a big, formal office with a marble floor partially covered by a dark green rug, a brass spittoon within easy shooting distance of the senator's desk. Norris asked only two or three questions, posed no objections to the changes, and sent them on to Lister Hill, the congressman for the Tennessee Valley district in Alabama. Because hearings had already been held on the earlier bill, the leadership on Capitol Hill, caught in a glut of new legislation, put the TVA bill to a vote without hearings or debate, and it passed without much dissent. In fact the process moved so fast that the participants were not completely sure of who proposed what, and of what had actually happened. Certainly Norris had a central role as chairman of the Agriculture and Forestry Committee in the Senate. (It was Norris who had stopped Henry Ford at Muscle Shoals a decade earlier. From 1921, when Wilson Dam at Muscle Shoals was completed, until 1931, Norris had introduced seven bills to create a public power agency at Muscle Shoals, and twice they were passed, only to be vetoed, by Calvin Coolidge in 1928 and finally by Hoover). By the time Roosevelt read his message to Congress on April 10, 1933, the administration's approach, as crafted by Gutheim and elaborated by a dozen others, had become much more comprehensive than Norris's earlier single-use proposals.

For Roosevelt, TVA was an engine of progress that could transform the most impoverished part of the country into one of the most prosperous. In December 1932, just after the election, he began to plan his strategy with Delano and Tugwell to gain popular support for the project. Roosevelt later wrote, "In enlarging the Muscle Shoals scheme so as to make it cover the whole Tennessee Valley, Senator Norris and I undertook to include a multitude of human activities and physical developments.... It touches and gives life to all forms of human concerns." In the 500,000 homes served by the Alabama Power Company in December 1932, there were a total of 85 electric sewing machines, 185 vacuum cleaners, 645 refrigerators, 700 radios. On the farms in the rural areas of Alabama and Tennessee, only one family in every 25 had electricity. After TVA appropriations were funded, Rep. John Rankin of Mississippi observed that "TVA is the most profitable investment the American people made since the Louisiana Purchase."

Among the many contributors to Roosevelt's interest in planning—including his wife, Eleanor; Theodore Roosevelt; and Gifford Pinchot—Delano was critically important. As the youngest railroad president in the nation, Frederic Delano began his career by walking the entire length of the Wabash System to survey the condition of its rail beds. One can easily picture him a few years later escorting his 11-year-old nephew Franklin through the 1893 World's Columbian Exposition, extolling the virtues of an architecture that was integrated into a grand scheme, as well as the inspirational merit of classical form. Later Delano presided over the Regional Plan Association of Chicago and raised funds to help persuade Daniel Burnham to devote the remainder of his career to the Chicago Plan. He supported the National Planning Board (through its various name changes as the National Resources Board in 1934, the National Resources Committee in 1935, and the National Resources Planning Board in 1939) until it was finally eliminated through the efforts of Senator Robert Taft in 1943.

It is not surprising that Franklin Roosevelt followed Delano's lead in these matters. The Beaux Arts colonnade of arched spillways of Wilson Dam at Muscle Shoals or the rigid academic classicism of Cass Gilbert's Supreme Court building were models for their brand of public architecture, a form that was translated into the Jefferson Memorial in Washington and hundreds of post offices and federal courthouses across the country during the New Deal years. Roosevelt met with Delano and his staff once a month to initiate great regional developments in other parts of the country, at Boulder Dam and along the Missouri and Columbia rivers.

Traveling from his "little cottage" in neighboring Warm Springs, Georgia, Franklin Roosevelt, his daughter Anna, Senator Norris, and other elected officials arrived in Muscle Shoals with an army of reporters and photographers. Roosevelt came to fulfill a campaign promise to visit the area and to see for himself the federal facilities—Wilson Dam, the nitrate plants and power stations, "the largest electric factories in the United States"—that would form the basis for his first great legislative initiative as president, the formation of the Tennessee Valley Authority. "I will put Muscle Shoals back on the map," declared Roosevelt before leaving the area.

Roosevelt named three men to sit as TVA's triumvirate. The chairman, Arthur E. Morgan, was an engineer and educator, as well as a Unitarian minister. He had managed a large flood control project from Memphis earlier in his career, followed by a similar project in the Miami Valley in Ohio, where he had become president of Antioch College. He was a self-made midwestern individualist and a pure Progressive. Soon after taking up his post in Knoxville (while retaining his position at Antioch), Morgan declared his intentions for TVA: "We are looking to a valley inhabited by happy people, with small hand-work industries, no rich centres, no rich people, but everybody sharing in the wealth."

The second appointee was David Lilienthal, a Progressive in the Woodrow Wilson mold. Also a midwesterner, he had gone to Harvard and then joined the Wisconsin Public Service Commission in 1931. Supreme Court Associate Justices Louis Brandeis and Felix Frankfurter (who taught public utilities law at Harvard and had been Lilienthal's mentor) recommended the 35-year-old Lilienthal to Roosevelt as the best and brightest in the field of utilities regulation. Finally, Harcourt A. Morgan, a Ph.D. in agriculture, already in Knoxville at the University of Tennessee, was appointed. Each of the three brought a different perspective to the meaning and promise of TVA. Roosevelt gave little hint as to what he wanted.

Arthur Morgan, who later wrote a biography of the utopian Edward Bellamy, had, according to Arthur Schlesinger, Jr., "a prophet's passion to achieve an integrated social and economic order." He was also an adviser to Eleanor Roosevelt, who had read his 1930 book, *A Compendium of Antioch Notes*, and was impressed by his ideas of developing cottage industries of home crafts, as she had done at Valkill near her home in Hyde Park and would do at Arthurdale in West Virginia. Lilienthal was more a businessman than an idealist. His agenda was to insure cheap power throughout the Valley, and he was willing to condemn property, flood farms and whatever else was necessary to attract industry. Both Arthur Morgan and Harcourt Morgan were sensitive to feelings of helplessness experienced by the many who had lost their land to the development of TVA progress. Harcourt Morgan, whose oversight was agriculture and forestry, was concerned that local voices would be drowned out by outside planners. By 1936 Arthur Morgan thought that there was "increasing danger that the electrical and water dam side of the project will swamp what may loosely be called the humanitarian side.... Cheap electricity is fine and desirable, but saving and reconditioning human lives is far more vital."

The early days of TVA can be viewed as a live, practical exercise in the ideas, principles, and designs of Mumford and the New York planners and of Frank Lloyd Wright. For Mumford, who was left on the sidelines as Roosevelt assembled his TVA team, the experience was embittering. "The RPAA group were unbelievably and completely naive. They thought that Roosevelt would simply call them up and ask for help [with TVA]," Gutheim recounted. For the Southern Agrarians in Nashville, TVA was a mixture of Yankee imperialism and a godsend for a region that had been devastated by a series of failed crops, declining land values, and years of little or no farm credit. In an interview with *The Washington Post* in 1934, Arthur Morgan explained how small communities empowered individuals, a principle of the Southern Agrarians: "An individual would divide his time between scientific farming and decentralized industry, preferably light industry.... The mountain regions of the South are the last bulwarks of individuality in America.... The 'Southern Highlander' is different. He likes rural life.... [He is] often regarded as merely cheap labor to be exploited, rather than a representative of a valuable type of culture to be encouraged and protected." Although the cross-currents are difficult to trace, it is Gutheim's opinion that "Wright was stimulated by what the government was doing and tailored his prejudices to the possibility of getting work." Taking a wider view, the intersection of ideas for decentralization—Wright's Broadacre plan, Mumford's fourth migration, Al Smith's and Roosevelt's regional planning initiatives, the regionalism conference at Charlottesville, and the manifesto by the Vanderbilt group—all point to Henry Ford and his 1922 plan for Muscle Shoals. With the credibility of celebrity, wealth, and power, and with Thomas Edison at his side, he had proposed to bring a utopian dream into the realm of the possible, inspiring visionaries who understood the possibilities and constructed a variety of similar, yet differing scenarios from Ford's outline. Because Ford's plan was only a sketch, others began to fill in the missing pieces. As engineers and intellectuals contemplated the complexities of regional development, Frank Lloyd Wright focused where no one else was looking, creating a new physical form for what was later to become the principal pattern of residential development across the country.

5. AT TALIESIN

As Wright continued to develop Broadacre City and the Usonian house, he was faced with certain practical problems—the need for assistants in the studio, on the farm, and at the house and the need for an income to supplement the meager commissions of the Depression. The Taliesin Fellowship was a partial solution. It also provided a way to pass on the principles of organic architecture to the next generation. Finally, it was also a demonstration of the viability, value, and joy of communal living on the land.

Wright's first attempt at organizing a school followed on an experimental program at the University of Wisconsin. Alexander Meikeljohn, former president of Amherst College, came to the University of Wisconsin in 1925 to begin the Experimental College, a progressive coeducational program that combined a study of the Great Books with projects and readings in American studies. The sophomore reading list included Thoreau's *Walden*; Louis Sullivan's *Autobiography of an Idea*; *The Education of Henry Adams*; Jane Addams's *Twenty Years at Hull House*; and selections from Emerson, Sandburg, Twain, Whitman, Stuart Chase, Henry George, Thorstein Veblen, Frederick Jackson Turner, Arthur Meier Schlesinger, and Lord James Bryce. Students also read novels by Dos Passos, Sinclair Lewis, Melville, and O'Neill, and poetry by Frost, Dickinson, Whitman, and Dreiser. Government studies included readings in Brandeis, Holmes, Lincoln, Lippman, Woodrow Wilson, and La Follette. One important part of the program was a regional study that each student undertook over seven or eight months, spanning the freshman and sophomore programs. Wright proposed an industrial arts program to be founded by the university but located at Taliesin, and he circulated a sketch of the Hillside Home School of the Allied Arts (named for his aunts' school at Spring Green) to university faculty. Talks and correspondence with Glenn Frank, president of the university, ceased when Wright left for the Southwest to begin his project for Alexander Chandler. But at Ocotillo in the Arizona desert in 1929, Wright began to evolve a form from a set of principles that covered people and the processes of creation in addition to the products of design.

Olgivanna, more than anyone, encouraged Wright's sense that architecture began and ended as a way of life, not simply in the bricks and mortar of construction or the picture postcards of the finished work. Before she and Wright met she had lived as a disciple of Georgi Gurdjieff at his Institute for the Harmonious Development of Man at Fontainebleau, outside Paris, a community formed to practice Gurdjieff's regimen for bringing the human spirit into harmony with the earth.

Following what she had seen and learned from Gurdjieff, Olgivanna had a significant influence in shaping the Fellowship. The two communities were about the same size, with an average of about sixty people in residence. Gurdjieff and his guests lived in an area of the house known to those who didn't as "The Ritz," while all others lived in spartan accommodations, a situation not unlike Taliesin. Hard outdoor work—"adding tired to tired," as Wright would have said—was the daily routine in both communities, where the morning bell rang early, well before first light in winter. In addition, Olgivanna and her daughter Svetlana brought the whirling dervish dances of the institute to Taliesin, creating an active music program that continues to be an important part of the community. In 1931, the year before the Fellowship was organized, Olgivanna described Gurdjieff's institute in an article for *The Bookman*:

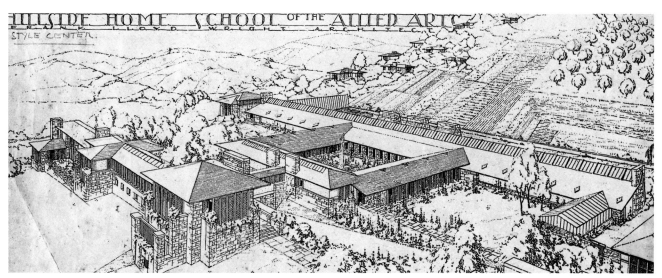

A 1928 perspective drawing by one of Wright's Taliesin assistants of the proposed Hillside Home School of the Allied Arts, with Wright's Hillside Home School building on the left and new construction on the right

There were doctors, painters, dancers, writers, musicians. All believed
that the possibilities of development, knowledge, and achievement are
much greater than those already achieved; that interior life—through
self-control, through identification with the ever-changing states of
one's being; through sacrifices, through never-tiring efforts to understand more and do more, through willingness to suffer more when
needed—can be made real, can be made even immortal....Just to be
completely developed human beings, to have our mind, emotions,
movement, body, mechanism, in well-proportioned order, is a difficult task. and most of us, indeed, are far from that.

So this, in short, was our work in the Institute and we were reaching it by way of ordinary life: in the gardens, in the kitchen, doing
housekeeping, farming, until the day's work to keep up the Institute
was done. In the evening we worked in movement, exercises, memo-
rizing, concentration....

Although Wright was following his instincts, philosophically he was in sympathy with the progressive

movement in American education. At the University of Chicago, Robert Hutchins, recruited as president in

1929 at the age of 30, established a Great Books program, not unlike what Meikeljohn had started earlier at

Wisconsin. John Dewey's ideas for progressive education spread from Chicago to other urban centers, such

as the New School for Social Research in New York (where Wright gave a series of lectures) and Columbia

Teachers College and later to experimental communities away from the city, like St. Johns College in

Annapolis, the Putney School, the Putney Graduate School of Education, and Bennington College in Ver-

mont, Bard College in New York state, Black Mountain College in the Smoky Mountains of North Carolina,

Berea College in Kentucky, and Antioch College in Ohio, all incorporating a varying mixture of experiential

education and liberal studies.

Progressive schools and experimental colleges were part of the utopian spirit of the 1930s, a commingling of idealistic optimism and practical education. Historian Charles Beard, who founded the New School in New York with John Dewey and was later a frequent visitor at Taliesin West, wrote in 1934 that "the next America would be a collectivist democracy—a workers' republic—one vast park of fields, forests, mountains, lakes, rivers, roads, decentralized communities, farms, ranches, and irrigated deserts…a beautiful country—homes

The Wrights on a picnic at Taliesin, 1955

beautiful; communities and farms beautiful; stores and workshops beautiful.… Sheer Utopianism, my masters will say…but let it be clearly understood then that there are elements of Utopianism in all of us."

Another stream of influence at Taliesin, Wright's denunciations notwithstanding, was the Bauhaus, although the German school was more a fellowship of equals than Taliesin, which was organized around a master-apprentice relationship. When it was closed by the Nazis, the Bauhaus disappeared in Europe, re-emerging at Harvard under Gropius and at the Armour Institute under Mies in Chicago. Earlier communities based on the practice of arts and crafts, such as C. R. Ashbee's Guild and School of Handicraft at Chipping Campden in Gloucestershire and Elbert Hubbard's Roycroft Shops in East Aurora, New York, were also precedents, as were even earlier communitarian settlements such as Robert Owen's New Harmony, Indiana; Joseph Smith's Nauvoo, Illinois; and the Amana communities of Iowa.

When organizing Taliesin, Wright sounded out a number of candidates to lead his "school," including Meikeljohn, Mumford, and Henrik Wijdeveld from Holland, publisher of *Wendingen*, who almost took the job but backed out at the last minute because of the state of Wright's finances. In the end, the Wrights, as usual, did everything themselves, along with a few of the "Taliesin men" who predated the Fellowship— Robert Goodall, Karl Jensen, Henry Klumb with his wife Else, Rudi Mock, and Samuel Ratensky.

Early Taliesin apprentices helped to convert Hillside Home School into a drafting room and other facilities. (From left) Eugene Masselink, Benjamin Dombar, Frank Lloyd Wright, Edgar Tafel, and John Howe, c. 1934

Looking for support, funding, and students, Wright took out his address book and solicited help and interest from everyone he knew and beyond. The "Friends of the Fellowship" included almost the whole *New Yorker* stable of writers, architects from Europe and the U.S.—Gropius, Mendelsohn, Buckminster Fuller, Mies, Kahn, Oud, and Bruce Goff— and musicians, artists and writers from everywhere, Edward Steichen and Alfred Stieglitz, Georgia O'Keeffe, Carl Sandburg, and Leopold Stokowski. Family members and Frank Lloyd Wright, Inc.

investors subscribed, along with Albert Einstein, John Dewey, and dozens of others.

The number of charter apprentices, first projected at 70, was revised downward by Wright, with 35 men and women in place on October 25, 1932, when Henry Klumb prepared a list for a Fellowship brochure. Seven were listed as college graduates, including Elizabeth Bauer from Vassar and Yen Liang, who had come from Peking to attend the University of Pennsylvania. John (Jack) Howe and Willets Burnham (a grand-nephew of Daniel Burnham), coming directly from Chicago area high schools, were perhaps the youngest members. The rest came from colleges across the country, including Abrom Dombar from the University of Cincinnati, William Beye Fyfe from Yale (whose father, James Fyfe, was Herman von Holst's partner, and whose mother, Hannah Beye, was matron of honor at a Wright's sister's wedding), William Wesley Peters from MIT, and Edgar Tafel from New York University.

The first projects at Taliesin for the young apprentices were construction, building their own housing and other facilities to accommodate a much bigger Taliesin family. According to Edgar Tafel, most of the projects in the drafting room for the new apprentices were exercises. "I redrew rooms of the Imperial Hotel and an elevation of St. Marks-in-the-Bouwerie." There was only one house on the drawing boards, a house for Nancy and Malcolm Willey of Minneapolis.

"I have just finished your book (the autobiography)...cover to cover," Nancy Willey began in her June 27, 1932, letter to Wright, admitting, "I have little hope you would take on anything so trivial." She described their lot, ample ground with a vista spanning three-quarters of the horizon, a daylight view of the Mississippi River on the left, a night view of city lights twinkling through the trees on the right. On July 5, Wright replied,

"Nothing is trivial because it is not 'big,'" accepting the commission and inviting the Willeys to visit him at Spring Green. By the next week, Nancy Willey, traveling alone by bus, arrived at Taliesin, "a wonderful world...mystical...it was interesting everywhere I looked," she recalled six decades later. Soon afterward, she sent Wright a $75 retainer, enclosing a note, "We appreciate very much your being so kind to our small idea."

Wright's first design for a house for Malcolm and Nancy Willey. The bedrooms, below the living room balcony and parapet, would have had views of the Mississippi River during the winter.

Miraculously, the preliminary plans for a two-story house were on their way to the Willeys by August 11, with a prediction from Wright that bids would not be greater than the budget of $8,000–$10,000. The Willeys were not rich. They had met ten years before. Nancy, who had graduated from Barnard in 1923, was from Brooklyn and had spent her summers at a family cottage at Sag Harbor on Long Island, an indoor-outdoor place she had always loved. Malcolm, from rural Connecticut, was getting his Ph.D. in sociology at Columbia when they married. Willey grew up with a grandfather who had been an associate of Horace Greeley at the *New York Tribune* and a family that owned a country newspaper, the subject of his dissertation. In 1924 he began teaching at the University of Minnesota, taking a leave to lecture at the University of Chicago, the Valhalla of liberal studies, for 1929–30 and for a stint in Washington in 1931 as investigator and as author of a report for the President's Research Committee on Recent Social Trends, an effort that was transformed into the National Planning Board when Roosevelt replaced Hoover in the White House. Later Willey became dean, then academic vice president, of the University of Minnesota.

The house Wright designed followed a plan he had first used for a house for the Avery Coonleys, that is, having a raised, second-story living room, an "upside down house," as the *Minneapolis Star* called it. The Willey plan was spacious, with garage, two bathrooms, servant's quarters, and a wide-open balcony overlooking the Mississippi. By November, bad news arrived: bids for the house were double the budget. After Thanksgiving, Wright wrote to Nancy Willey: "We'll try again. It seems the simplest way." The second try took a year. First the Willeys were beset by family illnesses which diverted their attention for several months. Wright, busy with building projects at Taliesin—a new large skylit drafting room and a theater, the Taliesin Fellowship

Complex at Hillside—probably assumed that the Willeys had simply dropped the project. In any event, almost a year passed before Nancy Willey tried again, requesting a "drastic simplification" of the plans:

"I do not want a seventeen thousand dollar house even at twelve or ten thousand dollars, " she wrote to Wright on November 26, 1933.

> I want an eight to ten thousand dollar house at eight to ten thousand dollars. Can I have it? What I mean is this: if I could put the bricks down myself side by side and with my Herculean efforts help to build the house I would indeed rise to the challenge, for I am very much in love with it too. But I can't do that. I am only a client and, as far as I can see, the only Herculean efforts a client can make are in the nature of shouldering obligations greater than one wanted in the first place, a role which I feel is a mean one and in the end would poison the joy in the house itself. We place such a high value on having a Frank Lloyd Wright house that we are unwilling to poison our joy in it by having too large a debt on it, and we will always feel that way.

Six weeks later, sketches for a new house were sent to Minneapolis. "Mr. Willey is thrilled and so am I. Our friends say that they like it better than the first house. Perhaps they can understand better poetry in houses than drama. I was pleased when my best friend said it was the most beautiful house she had ever seen." The cost of the second Willey scheme, it appeared, was right on target. Having a client with a fixed budget in the midst of the Depression forced Wright to abandon "drama" for "poetry," as Nancy Willey so elegantly put it. Through winter and spring, she conferred with, cajoled, and corralled the contractor and suppliers as the project's superintendent. When $30 brick was proposed, she found $8 brick. Little by little, the budget came within reach. By spring thaw, they were ready.

At the end of March Malcolm finally joined Nancy for his first visit to Taliesin. Her impressions of that weekend were particularly vivid. "We were so graciously received," she remembered in 1989,

> and Taliesin was so impressive: long, low dark corridors, opening to great vistas...the place was so mysterious—low to the ground, winding pathways through rocks and gardens. There were deep traditions at Taliesin. Clearly, Wright loved living in his ancestral valley, loved looking up at the Romeo and Juliet windmill.... Mrs. Wright was lovely and beautiful, and almost as impressive as he was....The whole that Taliesin embraced—the architecture, Mrs. Wright, the apprentices, the lovely buildings, the ambiance, the celebrity and the modesty of the place were just breathtaking. My first love might have been Taliesin.

On Sunday they were invited into the master's inner sanctum to discuss details of their project. In fact, they talked only about Broadacre City, with drawings for its master plan scattered about the studio and Wright enthusiastically presenting his sweeping ideas. The conversation must have been instructive to Wright as well as to Willey. The 1931 report that Willey had written for the White House, "The Agencies of Communication," had been sent to Wright by Nancy Willey. It contained, according to Lionel March, a strong advocacy for the automobile and argued convincingly that "localism" was promoted by the trend toward automobilization. But Willey's influence on Wright was probably more sweeping. He had blended communication and transportation issues into a single theme, concluding that "changes in the transportation system...[and] in point to point communication have similarly extended the radius of man's contacts," a fundamental concept in Wright's exposition of Broadacre City. Willey's 20,000-word report covered transportation systems, including railroads, trucks, and automobiles, highways and highway utilization, water and air transportation, and tourism; communications systems, including the postal service, telegraph, cable and wireless services, and the telephone, and how these services existed in a network; mass media, including newspapers and periodicals, motion pictures, and radio broadcasting, and their agencies of control. In its outline of trends, the Willey report provided Wright with a blueprint for the communication-transportation grid of the future that was undoubtedly incorporated into the Broadacre plan.

As they walked through the studio door to go to lunch, they stopped to read a sign posted on a bulletin board:

Lo! On the Horizon a Customer Appeareth. By God, He shall not Perish on this Earth.

"I wonder what rascal did that, " Wright, obviously embarrassed, said as they passed. The Willeys were astonished. "Our first surprise was that he accepted us as clients. Our second surprise was that he was in the midst of a school rather than working with clients, with telephones ringing, a busy celebrity at work. Instead we found that we were his only clients and that his work—Broadacre City—was all theoretical. He appeared as an estate farmer, at home, a place filled with music, surrounded by his students "

With that, Nancy Willey began to build her dream house, telegraphing Wright on May 1, "GROUND BROKEN TODAY. GIVE THREE CHEERS." With only one or two site visits from Edgar Tafel and Yen Liang, she went ahead, working with her contractor, firing off questions to Wright by mail almost daily, cautioning him as they broke ground to "please remember the Willeys will build anything you decide down to the last detail." The final details were handled by Wright's secretary, Gene Masselink, Tafel, and Liang, and the house was completed before the first snowfall.

John Sergeant describes the Willey house as transitional, since its "angled wide eaves, hipped roof, internally battened ceiling, and symmetrical planting boxes" were characteristic of Wright's earlier Prairie Style houses, while other features were Usonian. Its materials were cypress and brick, and it was the first of Wright's houses where the bricklayers were instructed that "horizontal joints [were] to be raked ¼" deep, leaving a concave joint, and vertical joints to be pointed up flush with the mortar colored to match the brick," a technique John Burroughs had advocated in 1886, later a standard feature of Usonian houses.

A precursor to the Usonian house, the Willey house was completed in 1933. The single-story plan combined a dining area with the living room and incorporated other features that would emerge as elements in Wright's Usonian concepts.

The balcony parapet of the first design for the Willeys was reminiscent of a number of Prairie Style houses that Wright designed in and around Chicago in the first decade of the century. Several of these were hillside houses, the spaces composed vertically, with the dining room and kitchen on the ground floor; entry, living room, and bedrooms on the second floor; and additional bedrooms on the third floor. With the first Willey design, Wright turned the plan upside down, placing the kitchen and living room together on top and the bedrooms below.

While the composition was more horizontal than in many of his earlier houses, it still relied on a compact, multistoried plan. With the second Willey plans, these ties were broken. Rooms were arranged horizontally, along a nearly straight line. In the first plan, the dining area was visually separated from the living room by a wall and placed on a slightly lower elevation. The kitchen became smaller and a pantry was eliminated. The first project contemplated a live-in housekeeper, with bedroom and bath opposite two identical bedrooms across the hall. The next plan eliminated the housekeeper's room and bath, slightly enlarging the master bedroom. The garage of the early plan became a carport; as the study became smaller, bookshelves were placed in the hallway connecting living room to bedrooms. The kitchen adjoined the living/dining room, leaving no doubt that the Willeys' dinner parties would be prepared by the Willeys and not by servants. Outside, the large balcony parapet became a smaller, triangular terrace off the living room. In making this new design, Wright was able to reduce the cost substantially, finally making it feasible for the Willeys to build.

At some time before construction began the Willeys recommended to Wright H. G. Wells's 1901 classic, *Anticipations of the Reaction of Mechanical and Scientific Progress upon Human Life and Thought,* "in which he predicts the trends of the next 50 years with amazing accuracy, in all their stupidities; the part about home architecture is especially sharp." Indeed. Wells predicted the diffusion of the population into the countryside, with "wayside restaurants and tea houses, and motor and cycle stores...dotted at every convenient position along the new roads." Wells also predicted the "practically automatic house" for "scientifically trained" people, a new class whose occupation and skill would lead to an economical, efficient household, while the "leisure class" would be the "decorative influence in the State," maintaining reactionary standards for design.

Wells forecast the rise in historic preservation and antique collecting (women, he said, would "ransack the ages for becoming and alluring anachronisms" and would dominate the arts, buying up "almost all the available architectural talent"). The Willeys, a modern young couple from genteel families, were delighted with these Wellsian predictions, thinking of themselves in the vanguard of a new day.

Beginning with the Willeys, many of Wright's middle-income clients were surprised when Wright deigned to consider their patronage. From 1930 to 1935, Wright experimented with formulas devised to bring his organic architecture to this new group for whom his ideas had appeal, men and women who read his autobiography, crowded into his lectures, and were impressed by thoughtful commentators who praised his work. The differences between the first and second Willey plans are indicative of both the problem and the solution: Wright, an architect known for his exuberance, as distinct from the austerity of the European and California modernists, required an expression that was both inexpensive and practical, yet completely consistent with his past work.

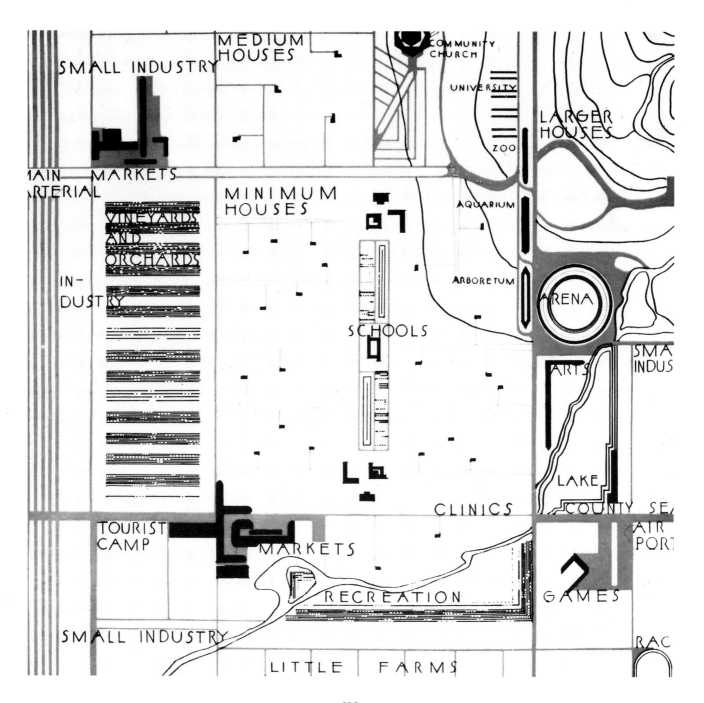

SMALL INDUSTRY

MEDIUM HOUSES

COMMUNITY CHURCH

UNIVERSITY

ZOO

LARGER HOUSES

MAIN ARTERIAL MARKETS

VINEYARDS AND ORCHARDS

IN-DUSTRY

MINIMUM HOUSES

AQUARIUM

ARBORETUM

ARENA

SCHOOLS

ARTS

SMA INDUS

LAKE

CLINICS

COUNTY SE

TOURIST CAMP

MARKETS

AIR PORT

RECREATION

GAMES

SMALL INDUSTRY

LITTLE FARMS

RAC

(Opposite) A detail of the plan for the Broadacre City model, constructed at Taliesin West in
1935

6. BROADACRE CITY

In November 1934 Edgar and Lillian Kaufmann visited their son Edgar, Jr., at Taliesin. After a Sunday night dinner, Wright expounded on his vision for Usonia and its realization in Broadacre City. He wanted to construct a model and tour the country, presenting an organic architecture that would complement his ideas for decentralization. Edgar Kaufmann was intrigued by Wright's proposal for new cities across the countryside and agreed to finance the project, writing a check for $500 on the spot as a down payment. Wright took the money and went to Madison, purchasing a big red truck from Orren Smart, his car dealer. By the end of the week, pieces for the Broadacre model were being jigsawed by apprentices while Wright made telephone calls to line up venues for his exhibit. He continued to refine Broadacre City as the model was constructed, moving the pieces around on the 12-by-12-foot platform, creating and recreating the composition as new forms were added. "Make me a half dozen St. Marks Towers," he said one morning to an assistant, artfully scattering them across the model's landscape when they arrived after lunch. The Fellowship first worked on the model in Wisconsin, moving on to Arizona after Christmas, where the Fellowship established a temporary working space at the stable of a winter resort in the desert.

When it was finished, the Broadacre City model represented four square miles accommodating 1,400 families. The arrangement of components across the 144-square-foot, 75-feet-to-an-inch model provided a neat and orderly vision to audiences assaulted by the jumble of ordinary urban landscapes. As a convenient device, Wright used the topographical map of Taliesin for the model's contours.

At Broadacre City everyone had space, at least an acre per family for house and car to a maximum of 10 acres for a farmer (the density of Raymond Unwin's garden city was 12 families to an acre). Interstate and intercity roads and local byways helped to separate little factories, farms, vineyards, and orchards from homes and shopping, while maintaining a close relationship between the two. Schools stood at the center of each concentration in Broadacre City, flanked by homes, then professional and governmental offices, a stadium, hotel, zoo, arboretum, library, community center, aquarium, arts center, and apartment houses, all surrounded by parks, streams, and flowering meadows bordered by trees. In the hills beyond lay luxury housing, a waterworks, forest cabins, a country club, and a center to train young architects ("Taliesin equivalent"). While the model was meant to be a piece of a continuous landscape, each area of the built environment formed a county seat. In later refinements of Broadacre City, Wright divided the then 48 states into a tristate Federal Union—Usonia, Usonia South, and New England—in which New England was essentially left alone as a trading and financial center. Usonia covered the country east to west with plans for the South differing to accommodate a greater emphasis on agriculture.

The organizing principle of Broadacre City was traffic control, reflecting Wright's view of the automobile as a wondrous machine, a rolling paradigm for the modern age, an icon of freedom. His arterial interstate

In rented winter quarters at La Hacienda, an Arizona resort, the Fellowship completed the Broadacre City model in sections that were transported in a pickup truck for an exhibition at Rockefeller Center in New York, April 1935.

road system included a center-lane monorail that traveled at 220 miles an hour. Motorcars traveled along 12 surface lanes and small trucks on parallel service roads. Below, tractor trailer trucks traveled on subterranean roadways, three deep in settled areas, with underground loading bays and warehouses. "Every Broadacre citizen has his own car," declared Wright. "There are no grade crossings nor left turns on grade. The road system and construction is such that no signals nor any lamp-posts need be seen. No ditches are alongside the roads. No curbs either. An inlaid purfling over which the car cannot come without damage to itself takes its place to protect the pedestrian." Wright also envisioned "aerotors," individual helicopters that could take off or land in a "hexacomb" or by "a doorstep if desired."

The sizes of Broadacre houses were defined by the automobile, and the display incorporated examples of "one-car," "two-car," and "five-car" houses. These represented pre-Usonian designs, including the House on the Mesa (designed for the International Style exhibition of 1932), the Davidson Farm Units (described in chapter 7), the Willey house, and a mix of other building forms that foreshadowed the Usonian house. "The

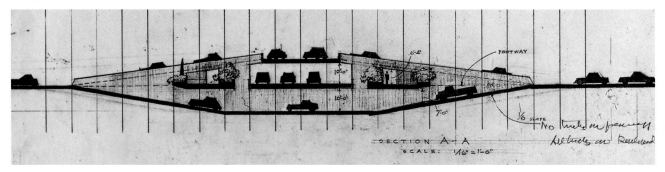

Broadacre City was designed around the automobile and the pesdestrian. In this "Plan of Minor Highway," Wright separated foot from motor traffic and further separated cars from trucks, pushing commercial vehicles underground and out of sight as they passed through settled areas.

houses of Broadacre City are varied in type and size," Wright explained. "Most of them are planned for construction with factory-fabricated units that permit varied room arrangements. They would also use prefabricated utility assemblies and all of them would have space for at least one automobile.... Many houses would [also] include facilities for professional activities. Thus a chemist would have a laboratory within his home, or a carpenter his workshop."

In every article, lecture, and interview, Broadacre City was presented as a transitional idea and a conceptual model rather than a specific plan, "the first...cross-section of a complete Civilization," according to Wright. Again and again, Wright spoke of Broadacre City as "everywhere and nowhere," a floating apparition reminding land developers and planners that the city and its fringes were doomed and that the salvation for development lay across the wide open spaces of the countryside. Decentralization was only the first principle of Broadacre City. Architectural integration was the second. For Wright, integration encompassed the whole of organic building and architecture: integration between site and building; integration of building methods, providing cost savings through on-site fabrication from standardized parts; integration of building materials across a landscape, creating rhythm without repetition; integration among transportation systems (including the use of highways as runways for aircraft); integration of "electrical intercommunications," including radio, telephone, and telegraph; integration of work, family life, farming, and recreation; and, of course, integration of people and environment, a city "designed as a broad-way into Democratic future-life for Usonians." The only powerful civil authority in Broadacre City was the county architect, a sort of benevolent architect-magistrate in Wright's image, trained in the principles of organic architecture.

The third principle of Broadacre City was the assertion of Jeffersonian individualism, which Wright felt had been obliterated by city life, poverty, and the "mobocracy" of popular taste. According to Norris Kelly Smith, "the ultimate importance of Broadacres lay in the fact that it was sprung from the wholly personal center of Wright's own mind." The great irony was that in the exercise of his own freedom in creating Broadacre City, he

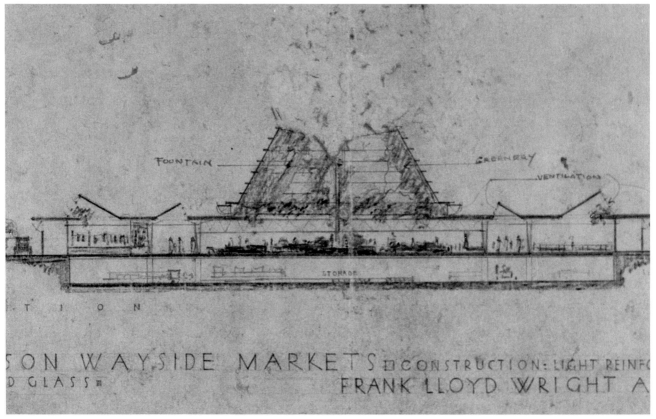

Davidson Wayside Markets, a 1932 concept developed by Wright as he began to create his ideas for Broadacre City. The design was a forerunner of the modern suburban shopping mall. It was planned for construction in light reinforced concrete, with an atrium beneath an enormous glass and copper roof.

was imposing his will on everyone else. As a singular vision, the Broadacre plan was a city writ new, without a past and frozen in time, without edges, without dissent, without the ability to grow or the danger of decline. Broadacre City's only history was in its buildings, which, in addition to houses, included the 1929 St. Marks-in-the-Bouwerie, the 1925 Gordon Strong Automobile Objective, and other unrealized projects from Wright's past.

The fourth principle of Broadacre City, a corollary to individualism, was Wright's perception of its appeal to urbanites searching for a sense of community. Perhaps the Taliesin Fellowship generated a greater communitarian spirit in Broadacre City than had existed in earlier Wright projects; or perhaps it was the spirit of Wright's generation, which had seen the rise of socialism in Europe. It is ironic that the artistic successor to François Fourier, a founder of socialism, was William Morris, whose Arts and Crafts movement rejected the machine age, and whose American followers, the Roycrofters in the East and Bernard Maybeck and the Greene brothers in the West, did not preach the establishment of intentional communities as did Wright.

Broadacre City was conceived in part as an escape from a purely capitalistic, currency-based economy. Ownership of land for Usonians in the Broadacre plan was not clearly explained, although a form of social credit, accrued as a right of citizenship, was part of the concept. Wright's views on economics, while not in the mainstream of the New Deal, were derived from policies being discussed at the time. His ideas on social credit, for instance, probably came directly from A. H. Orage, a British writer who became Georgi Gurdjieff's leading disciple and fund raiser in America in the 1920s and presumably came to Wright's attention through Olgivanna. By the early 1930s Orage had become a follower of Major Clifford Hugh Douglas, who espoused the socialization of credit to redistribute goods and wealth, ideas that were actually being tested in Alberta, Canada, at the time. Orage lectured in the United States on Douglas's ideas, offering solutions that soon were incorporated into Broadacre City: a citizen's right to a direct medium of exchange, a piece of ground, and a share in all inventions and scientific discoveries that benefited the Usonian nation. Wright was also intrigued by the ideas of Silvio Gesell, which were first introduced to him by Rudi Mock in the early 1930s, when Gesell's published theories for the elimination of money and the nationalization of land were available only in German.

To achieve a sense of security and community without urban densities, Wright proposed "little farms, little homes for industry, little factories, little schools, a little university," a cozy setting where the only thing big and powerful was the discretion of a benevolent county architect, trained in the principles of organic architecture. The concept of little farms and little factories was a direct descendant of Henry Ford's 75 Mile City at Muscle Shoals and his village industries program in Michigan. In fact, the example of the Bill Jones family cited by Littell McClung in his article in the September 1922 issue of *Scientific American*, describing 75 Mile City, would have fit perfectly into Broadacre City. But Wright's vision turned the seamless linear city of Ford's worker heaven into a sanctuary with a much larger middle-income component, and made it a place of architectural distinction. In the latter respect, Broadacre City was a great improvement on 75 Mile City, which was not proposed in any physical form. (If it had been, the architect probably would have been not Frank Lloyd Wright but Albert Kahn, Ford's factory architect, who eventually served as a consultant in the Tennessee Valley for several of the dams and for Norris Village, a conceptual successor to 75 Mile City.) As a practical man of industry and the largest private-sector employer in the United States, Ford never contemplated the Muscle Shoals concept as a complete replacement for the city, but only as an alternative direction for future development. But Wright, as an artist with a larger, yet impractical vision, presented Broadacre City as a total environment, an unending middle landscape that obliterated the confusion and clamor of the city, scattering its population from Chesapeake Bay into the desert of the Southwest.

At the exhibit's opening in New York, Wright broadcast a speech from Rockefeller Center, alienating with insults planners in Washington, the very constituency that he had sought to impress:

> The hope of Democracy has gone from bad to worse until almost no one believes the ideal practical. Here we are, a nation of "ites," "istic," with all the "isms" you ever heard of, inventing new ones and calling on the alphabet for salvation....

One social critic of the ideas contained in the exhibit, Stephen Alexander, observed in *New Masses*,

> Despite his badly confused notion of the nature of social forces in our society—(only a serious and completely sincere person could have written such a naive concoction of adolescent idealism and Wellsian it's-all-done-with-push-buttons fiction)—Frank Lloyd Wright must be regarded as one of the important forces in progressive American architectural thought....As far as relevance to an immediate program is concerned, the significance of Mr. Wright's project is that it points inexorably to the necessity for the removal of capitalism and the creation of a socialist society as the primary condition for the progressive development of architecture.

A few weeks later Wright replied to the *New Masses* editors that Broadacre City was anticapitalistic, anti-communist, and antisocialist. "Now all this dreaming may be too far ahead...I wish the world were not quite so callous and the people in it not [so] utterly sophisticated...."

A central question raised by the Broadacre City model and its concomitant explanations that spring in *Architectural Record* and *American Architect* was whether a middle-class community sited away from the economic forces of the city was a solution to the problems that America faced in the Depression. Wright's assertion of architecture as central to the American way of life was challenged by many social scientists, who believed that the realities of poverty and the links between consumption and production could not be grasped by either architects or engineers. As an inspiration Broadacre City had great potential appeal, particularly to people living in a depressed industrial city. The government's effort's in social planning were directed to providing a safety net for families living in substandard housing or in no housing at all. When Stephen Alexander called Broadacre City "a naive concoction of adolescent idealism," he was perhaps comparing it to actual projects—TVA, Robert Moses's efforts on Long Island and in Westchester County, New York, or the huge linear cities and collective farms being planned in the Soviet Union. In these and other large-scale plans, ideas dominated form, providing little that was actually new design. Wright's utopia committed not only to a layout, but to a whole series of newly articulated forms that worked both together and separately to create a seamless landscape of buildings, roadways, gardens, lakes, and streams, a lyric and a tune understandable without vaulted explanation.

Broadacre City was the vision of an artist-architect responding to both the economic chaos that surrounded him—a chaos that included disastrous effects on his opportunities to practice architecture—and to the flood of proposals and plans, government legislation and programs, books, articles, and speeches that analyzed, speculated, and projected solutions to social and economic problems that had eaten away America's self-confidence. Wright was perhaps the only private-sector architect in the country who was considering broadly defined social and economic factors as part of an architectural, rather than simply a planning, philosophy. Wright's ideas were both appealing and stimulating to their intended audience—professionals and intellectuals, men and women in journalism, the arts, and academia and on the fringe of public policy. But by rejecting suburbia, with its dependence on the city, Wright was also rejecting the web of power in local, state, and federal government that defined public discourse. As a consequence, Wright's influence on mainstream planning and public policy at the time was almost nil. Reaction from the building industry, business, and government was more bemused than solicitous. His ideas did, however, receive serious attention in the academic world.

In spring 1931, even before working on Broadacre City, Wright received an invitation to lecture from Baker Brownell, a professor at Northwestern University in Evanston. From Northwestern's Department of Contemporary Life and Thought, Brownell ran a lecture series that gave him access to a wide range of people influential in politics and intellectual life. Over the next several years Wright included Brownell's series in his schedule. The university paid $100–$200 for each visit, and Brownell provided Wright with introductions to men like Rexford Tugwell and Commander Eugene McDonald, the president of Zenith Radio, who "is just radical-minded enough...to want sometime to build a stimulating building...." By 1936 Brownell, whose principal activity was writing books, proposed a collaborative project between Wright, himself, and Paul

Douglas, a University of Chicago economist. The idea was to synthesize Broadacre City principles with social and economic planning into a practical prescription for the country and for Frederic Delano's National Resources Committee. Douglas dropped out of the project, but Brownell prepared a proposal, received Wright's approval, and made a contract with Harper and Brothers to deliver an 85,000-word manuscript. The result, published in 1937, was *Architecture and Modern Life*, by Baker Brownell and Frank Lloyd Wright, an amalgam of Wright's Broadacre City and Brownell's concepts for a distributive society. The book included a conversation between Wright and Brownell, recorded during one of Wright's visits to Evanston, after repeated attempts by Brownell to elicit manuscript copy from Wright.

Architecture and Modern Life is different from other Wright publications and books, a dialogue between a realist (Brownell) and a visionary (Wright). Although Brownell's publishing proposal probably no longer exists, it is evident from his correspondence that he presented *Architecture and Modern Life* as an annotated Wright, making the ideas and language of Wright accessible to a broader audience. Throughout the text, Brownell restates what Wright had presented in his Princeton lectures, his autobiography, and *The Disappearing City*. His commentary on Henry Ford in 1937 paraphrases Wright from 1930: "Mr. Ford has...broken up plants and distributed them among smaller towns...in an enlightened manner by making provision for the laborer to have a garden, a home, and part-time occupations outside his factory work, and at the same time retain good wages." His range of reference included regionalism, the Southern Agrarians, worker housing, big power, public transportation, the automobile, urban Judaism, progressive education, Lao-tzu, Ghandi, "prophetic artists" like regionalist painters (Grant Wood, Thomas Hart Benton, Edward Hopper) and regional writers (William Faulkner, Robert Frost, Carl Sandburg), modern music, and native American culture—each related to organic architecture. As Brownell saw it, Wright's mantra, "form and function are one," implied that the value of a design could be judged by its appearance. As a corollary, design must meet Wright's standards to be organic and have integrity. For Brownell, these definitions were too narrow, particularly for a civic architecture. While interpreting Wright to a larger public, he seemed to be interpreting and defending the larger culture to Wright.

Beyond issues of policy, Brownell was in love with the actual architectural forms that were taking shape at

Norris, Tennessee, built in 1936 near Norris dam, was conventional in layout and appearance yet was important in the effort to plan new communities that were economically self-sustaining.

Norris dam was an inspiration to Wright's coauthor Baker Brownell, who wrote that TVA was "building a civilization."

TVA. For Brownell, Norris Dam, the first dam designed and built by TVA after the 1933 legislation, was an impressive piece of civic architecture, "a wedge of concrete poured between two mountains." Norris integrated dam to site, coordinating dam, visitor center, village, roadways, and landscaping into a single idea, a meticulously executed demonstration of regional planning at its best. He was at least as impressed with Norris Village, a worker's Shangri-la with houses of four wood-paneled rooms, two porches, bath, shower, and fireplace, renting for $36 a month with all-electric cooking, heating, washing, refrigeration, and ironing at another $15–$20 in winter, $7–$10 in summer. Was this Usonia? To Brownell, TVA was "building more than a dam. It is building a civilization. The visitor here is looking into the next century."

When Norris was proposed, TVA first turned to the Bureau of Reclamation, which had designed the neoclassical Wilson Dam with the Army Corps of Engineers. When chairman Morgan asked the new TVA architect Roland Wank to comment on the bureau's sketches, the Austrian Wank countered with his own, a clean Viennese moderne design, an evolution from Adolf Loos and Otto Wagner, his Vienna mentors, who also trained Richard Neutra. For insurance, Morgan called in Albert Kahn, Henry Ford's factory architect, to review Wank's work. Kahn became a regular consultant, reviewing all TVA projects. (Years later, in an exchange with federal architect Talbot Wegg, Wright revealed that he considered Albert Kahn the best architect in the United States, after himself, of course.) Eventually, Wank left TVA to become chief of design for Albert Kahn Associates in Detroit.

Along with Roland Wank, Earle Draper, Jr., who came from Kingsport, Tennessee, and had been closely associated there with the senior John Nolen, was brought in to design Norris Village. When Draper was interviewed for the job of TVA's regional planning chief, he remarked to Chairman Morgan that TVA might do better with a firm like Olmsted in Boston. Morgan replied, "I don't want anybody coming in with an alien philosophy to try to tell us what to do.... [We need someone] who knows the South, has lived in the South, and can understand local conditions and won't be dominated by a clique or a group that [has] preconceived...notions of what has to be done down there."

Draper got the message. Early in his job, he stated, "TVA is not attempting to impose a new way of living upon the people of the Valley. Rather we attempt to blend modern forms with long-existing living habits and social customs of the locality." The blend was not always evident. In the large-scale public architecture—dams, power stations, laboratories, and visitor centers—the forms were monumental, with clean white surfaces, often framed by chrome or onyx trim, streamlining that looked more urban than rural, more European than American. In any event, by the time the first Norris designs were exhibited at the Museum of Modern Art in 1940, Arthur Morgan and others were persuaded that TVA civic architecture was "Americanism" at its best. Draper was a town planner, not a regional planner, and was concerned with the design of Norris Village, not a new society.

Through it all, from Norris to Wheeler to Pickwick, to later defense housing at Oak Ridge and experiments with prefabrication, Frank Lloyd Wright was not asked to contribute a single design, nor was Lewis Mumford asked to consult. When Mumford wrote about the dreadful condition of housing in America in 1932, he listed the seven conditions that must be met to achieve a successful program: comprehensive planning, large scale operations, mass production, efficient design, limited profits, cheap money, and state subvention for the poor. By the next year, all of these conditions were in place to test public housing on a grand scale in the Tennessee Valley. But again and again, the promise of regional planning in TVA was thwarted by limited vision and constraints of budgets, schedules, and politics.

To Mumford, the architecture of European public housing schemes was not suitable to the multicultural

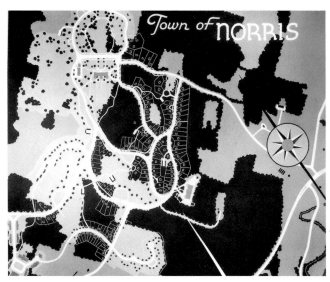

Site plan for Norris, Tennessee

society and varied terrain of the United States. Mumford thought that Frank Lloyd Wright, and perhaps only Frank Lloyd Wright, possessed the vision to create an architecture that bridged the differences. Later he singled out Wright's designs as "universal both in their origin and their destination, without for a moment losing esthetic contact with the place, the climate, the people for whom most immediately the building was created."

It is important to understand that before the Usonian house, there was no middle-class, middle-income house that could be considered to possess a style that was not part of another tradition. In fact, no one knew what exactly constituted an American style of architecture. Certainly neither Roland Wank, Albert Kahn, nor Earle Draper had the slightest idea what the blend of "modern forms" with "social customs of the locality" should look like.

Earlier in his career, Wright designed his great retreats—Taliesin, Midway Gardens, the Imperial Hotel— each with distinctive characteristics that were closely related to site, environment, culture, and region. Beginning with the second Willey house, he moved away from regionalism to the achievement of a generic concept, a house for all seasons in all American places, its variations based on the needs and personalities of its occupants and the particularities of its site, but seemingly not on the past traditions of its place. The assumptions of public architecture of the 1930s ran completely counter to these ideas. Since there was no original American architecture to rely on, the government architect's only option was an ersatz regionalism that interpreted usual and familiar building types, whatever their origins, as a way of blending into the environment, whether rural, suburban, or urban.

As a prototype for America, TVA was trumpeted by Roosevelt and everyone else down the line as an opportunity to achieve the universal, a chance to demonstrate the efficacy of planning as the salvation for democracy. Wright created Broadacre City as an environment to site his architectural ideas, giving birth to what became the Usonian house. Although he had the vision, he did not have the practical means to achieve universality. Wright's genius and weakness was his inability and unwillingness to follow conventional practices. Because of his arrogance and assertion of his individuality, Wright's personality and methods were incompatible with bureaucracies and public financing, and excluded collaborative problem solving and the other skills necessary to carry out the kind of public architecture required by TVA. He was not a man of business and did not respect the processes that government required. At the same time, and because of his idiosyncrasies, Wright's solution in the search for a universal form for the American dwelling proved to be completely original, and in the end, more enduring than it might have been if he had compromised with the government's procedures or been influenced by its preoccupations.

7. HOUSES AND HOUSING

When plans for a Frank Lloyd Wright Prairie Style house were first published in *Ladies' Home Journal*—"A Home in a Prairie Town" in February 1901 and "A Small House with 'Lots of Room in It'" in July 1901—he was contributing to a pioneering series on the small house for the most popular magazine in the world. Edward Bok, a Dutch immigrant and the *Journal*'s editor, believed in women's traditional role, but in the realm of domestic architecture he had progressive ideas, including the elimination of "senseless ornamentation" and the modernization of kitchens and bathrooms. He frequently published plans for houses costing $1,500 to $5,000, providing his readers by mail with complete working drawings and specifications for $5 a set. He helped popularize the bungalow, a ubiquitous form for the American small house from the turn of the century well into the 1930s. Stanford White remarked that Bok had "more completely influenced American domestic architecture for the better than any man in his generation."

As Bok and others continued to publish designs for small dwellings, the need for an architect for the design of individual houses diminished. By the mid-1920s, and with the dawn of modernism in America's consumer culture, some business leaders looked at what was going on in Europe and concluded that the industrialization of housing in the United States could follow the principles of Ford's Model T, combining modern design, new materials, prefabrication, and efficient construction methods to create a boom in housing across the country. A true believer in and promoter of these developments was Henry R. Luce, the young publisher of *Time* and *Fortune.*

In *Housing America*, published in 1931, the editors of *Fortune* presented housing as an obvious candidate for a new industrial enterprise. According to their view, houses could be turned out in cookie-cutter fashion and dropped onto any plot of land as a way of providing a national solution to local problems. Many disagreed, including Mumford, who believed that manufactured housing had completely different requirements from the automobile assembly line. Housing required public utilities and other communal facilities, in addition to land.

To further his interests in housing and construction, Luce announced in the April 11, 1932, issue of *Time* his purchase of *Architectural Forum* magazine: "The several elements of the building world—architects, engineers, contractors, workmen, investors—are at last integrating into a great industry...[and as an] early advocate of that integration, *Architectural Forum* promises to be the leading chronicler of a revolution in construction in the next decade." *Forum*'s previous publisher and owner, Howard Myers, was retained, along with his managing editor, Ruth Goodhue, who had become interested in European architecture while studying child psychology in graduate school in Vienna and Munich. With the introduction of Mies, Gropius, and Le Corbusier to the American public at the Museum of Modern Art's International Style exhibition in 1932, *Forum* quickly followed with major portfolios on the architecture of a dozen European countries, a series produced in Europe that ran in the magazine for over two years. By 1935 Myers had given himself the additional title of editor in chief and began more aggressively to promote architects practicing in the United States, including Richard Neutra, William Lescaze, the Pereira brothers, and William Wurster. Myers and Luce also paid particular attention to Frank Lloyd Wright, whose work and ideas began to appear regularly in *Forum* and whose antics and wisecracks became one of the continuing news stories covered by *Time*.

With virtually no building going on in the United States, the time could not have been more inauspicious for the purchase and relaunching of an architecture magazine. Yet Luce, who had been interested in architecture and construction for some time, recognized that the pent-up demand for new building would eventually be unleashed. Indeed, the New Deal launched $3.3 billion in construction programs as Luce's first issue of *Forum* was published. Two months later, the *Forum* staff created an 18-page special section on the new legislation, providing detailed instructions for architects and contractors on how to qualify for bidding on projects, a service to their readers that continued throughout the Depression years. Myers also regularly published plans for small houses, offering complete sets of construction drawings by mail, following the lead of Edward Bok of an older generation and reaching for an audience in middle America, where everyone without a house dreamed of having one.

■

"The small-house problem has invaded us again at Taliesin," wrote an apprentice in the August 30, 1934, weekly "At Taliesin" column appearing in the *Wisconsin State Journal*:

> The Small House—price ranging between $3,500 and $5,500—has been one of the most neglected architectural fields. The "big architect" could not make a living building small houses, so his thought has run to other directions. But now, there is a definite need for careful study of the small house. This is the only type of work there is for the architect, since the era of plenty has vanished. He can make it worthwhile if he thinks along the new line of thought, not only from the financial standpoint, but beauty as well. We have only to look at the new Tennessee Valley projects to see a new 1934 architectural blunder. These architects flooded the valley with a poor offshoot of the worn-out Colonial style; the style that is neat and clean looking, which in reality is a continuous "swipe." It always borrows. This Colonial house, painted white, with lovely pea green shutters that are never used, sells for $3,500 on long-term credit. Cheap enough. But what about its functioning? Its relation to the terrain? Its workability for the family? Its growth? Its materials? These phases have been sadly neglected.

Wright could complain about the houses in Draper's Norris Village, but he had no workable alternative to offer. Before the Willey house—which was site-specific and cost more than three times the Norris houses—Wright had designed a number of low-cost dwellings, but the generic solutions of his early years had found few paying customers. He experimented with his own house in 1889, then designed variations of his *Ladies' Home Journal* houses for Joseph Walser in Chicago (1903), Mrs. Thomas H. Gale in Oak Park (1904, built in 1909), Stephen M. B. Hunt in La Grange, Illinois (1907), G. C. Stockman in Mason City, Iowa (1908), and L.

K. Horner in Chicago (1908). Around 1915 he developed a prefabrication scheme for houses that he called American System Redi-Cut structures, and a few were built in 1916 in Milwaukee. But after his return from Japan, the only small house he actually built was La Miniatura (1923) for Alice Millard in Pasadena, the first of four textile-block houses he designed in the Los Angeles area.

In 1931 Wright had designed a small, nonurban factory worker's home that doubled as a small farm unit, following Henry Ford's ideas. One of the clients for his 1903 Larkin Building in Buffalo, Walter V. Davidson, had commissioned Wright to design small, prefabricated farming units, inspired, presumably, by Ford's Muscle Shoals scheme. For Davidson, Wright designed a series of buildings of sheet steel, a farm-in-a-kit, complete with a three-bedroom house attached to a farm building. As the commission immediately preceding the Willey house, the Davidson farmhouse presented the first example of a Usonian house plan, with a small kitchen work space next to the living room and a dining alcove. Although never built, the Davidson "Little Farms Unit" continued to evolve after the first February 1932 drawing, under slightly different legends, until it was used five years later as the farm manager's house for a planned (but unbuilt) project at Wingspread, Herbert F. Johnson's estate in Racine, Wisconsin. Along the way, Wright also designed a "Little-Farms Tract" for Davidson, a site plan for farms, a city hall, sewage plant, and other public facilities, an early exercise for Broadacre City. During this time he was working on other projects that informed the solution to the small house problem, including rough sketches for projects he called "The Norm for the Prefabricated House," "Conventional House," and, in 1934–35, the "Zoned House for City, Suburb and Country" and Broadacre City's "Subsistence Homestead."

The problem with developing the ideal small house for America was the lack of a ready client. Although Broadacre City was speculative, Wright rarely if ever designed buildings without a patron. To his mind, the Willeys were too affluent, too urban, their site too atypical to offer the right conditions for the prototypical house. Indeed, he was hardly thinking about "the small house problem" as he designed the first Willey house, which bid out at $17,000. Clearly he made a distinction between clients like the Willeys—educated, urbane, progressive—and the kind of client who would live in a $3,500 house in Muscle Shoals or in Norris Village.

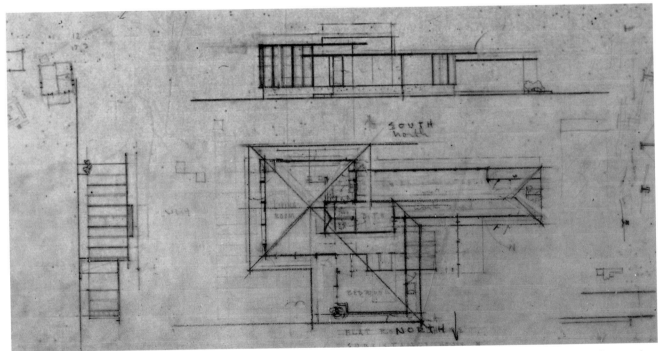

Wright experimented with various solutions for a low-cost house that led to his first Usonian houses. The plan and elevation of his "Broadacre City Subsistence Homestead," November 1934, were refined for the Hoult and Lusk houses the following year.

Indeed, Wright's reputation as an architect for clients with large, even unlimited budgets put him outside the league of architects attempting mass housing. Perhaps a larger problem was the perception that Wright was a master of customization who tailored each design to the requirements and aspirations of individual clients. Universal, assembly-line design—teams of architects working on mass housing—was anathema to Wright, who had never attempted to design at the lowest possible cost or with the least number of variables. As a practical matter, the question was whether Wright's original ideas for middle-income houses would be acceptable to mortgage lenders and their inspectors, who relied almost entirely on guarantees provided by the Federal Housing Authority. As if on cue, two clients appeared to test the waters, the Hoults of Wichita, Kansas, and the Lusks of Huron, South Dakota.

When Louise Hoult first contacted Wright in February 1935, the Fellowship was at La Hacienda in Chandler working on the Broadacre models. However theoretical Broadacre City was intended to be, the plan required a thoughtful architecture for a small house that was affordable to middle-class families, that is, a house costing about $5,000 in 1935 dollars (about $150,000 today). Gene Masselink responded to her letter promptly, indicating that a "four thousand dollar house [as she requested] would take a special study which Mr. Wright is interested to take up." After the addition of a second bath and third bedroom to the program, the budget was revised to $5,500, and Wright proceeded with plans on the understanding that Mr. Hoult, who was in the building supply business, would be able to buy all of the materials for the house at wholesale cost.

By August plans were completed and a model had been built. In a letter to Louise Hoult, Masselink called the house "a fresh projection of a really significant idea into architecture." In this case, the architect was well ahead of the clients. A year after their first letter, the Hoults still had not come to Taliesin to see the model and had not selected a site for their house (although they owned a farm and had considered locating the house there). After a round of changes requested by the Hoults, Wright revised the plan and provided new preliminary drawings on March 17, 1936. Masselink detailed the construction approach: "wide boards and battens...stained for protection and banding the house into rhythmic patterns," chimney stack, the related wall piers, and flower boxes in brick also containing kitchen and bath, built-in illumination. The layout was designed "upon a rectangular unit system—4 foot by 2 foot 2 inches—with all the rooms opening onto a courtyard." Masselink continued, "The dining room is an extension of the living room and is in convenient relation to the kitchen which is sunlit and aired from above. The bedrooms are located in a separate wing.... The car port is minimized.... Wardrobes in the bedrooms are...built-in.... The roof is a new system of construction.... No plaster is used.... The inside walls throughout are to be covered with Nu-wood left 'natural'...."

"This is a plan that can grow," said Masselink, mindful that the Hoults were a growing family. In almost every detail, the Usonian house was created for the Hoults. One result of the Hoult job was the beginning of the Standard Detail Sheet—what Wright called a Usonian "grammar"—that provided details of a through-the-wall section he used, with only minor variations, for each of the Usonian successors to the Hoult house. But as in so many projects, specifications for a $4,000 budget that became $5,500 brought in estimates of $10,000, making it impossible for the Hoults to proceed. As Wright solved one design problem after another, a solution to the cost factor was elusive.

A second attempt to produce a small house on a limited budget was made for the Lusk family in Huron, South Dakota. When newspaper publisher and editor Robert D. Lusk first contacted Wright in 1935, he was helping to promote a project to replace a resort hotel, which had burned to the ground, at Sylvan Lake in Custer State Park in the Black Hills. Faced with a competition for the hotel's design, Wright demurred (as he always did when asked to design without a commitment from a client), dismissing the opportunity on general principles. The hotel was to be financed with federal funds from the Works Projects Administration, and the state's governor and senior senator were willing to intercede to prevent the park board from retaining the services of the National Park Service's architecture department. Lusk wrote to Wright to persuade him to join in the process: "Were these...people to be shown a preliminary drawing of the type of hotel you would build at Sylvan—the conception which you had when you stood on the crags back of the present hotel—I cannot imagine any other result than that they would appreciate the difference between the run-of-the-mill architect and a Frank Lloyd Wright."

In January 1936, after plans for the hotel project went forward without Wright, Lusk wrote to request plans for a house. "The location is far from exciting. This is...a flat country.... There is nothing very attractive about [this] small prairie town," he wrote. Lusk indicated his desire for a "very small" house, having a "living room big enough for piano, entertainment of guests, etc. We would like a small library or den with some desk space and considerable book space and with a fireplace. We would like a dining room, and, of course, a kitchen. We want two, and if possible, three bedrooms. In the basement...a recreation room, a laundry, and storage and furnace space...." Then Lusk added a request inspired by a visit to the Willeys in Minneapolis, "Oh, yes, I might add here that I have a strong aversion against having the living room and dining room together." The plans for the Lusk house were in the mail a week before the second Hoult plan, March 10, 1936.

In the end the Lusks were unable to obtain financing. In a 1973 letter to John Sergeant, Jeannette Lusk recalled, "Government loans were about the only source of funds in those days, and we couldn't build without one. The FHA declared that because our house was 'different,' ... had been designed specifically for us and our personal requirements and way of life, that its re-sale value was nil. The Government had to figure in the resale value because many builders receiving loans defaulted on their payments."

While the Hoult and Lusk houses were on the drawing boards, the Fellowship was hard at work on the Broadacre City model. In important ways, the work on one complemented the other. The grid on which Broadacre City was laid out followed closely the grid of these first Usonian houses, the first scaled to a land-

Living and dining areas in the Hoult house (left) and Lusk house (right) were conceived as single, flowing spaces. This view appears in a very similar perspective rendering for the 1936 Jacobs house and the 1939 Rosenbaum house. See page 144.

scape, the latter to a building site. The zones for Broadacre City activities—traffic, education, recreation, community gatherings, commerce—are reflected in the layout of the Usonian house, with a distinct car parking arrangement and with gathering places distinct from private or sleeping spaces, food preparation and other work spaces delineated from areas for social intercourse. These first Usonian houses also helped Wright to articulate a design for single-family living on the middle landscape, a place without the rural wide open spaces for his Davidson Farm Unit but with ample ground to accommodate the long, low horizontal wings of his Usonian dwellings.

A few days after Wright presented the city that was everywhere and nowhere to New York, Franklin Roosevelt signed an executive order creating the Resettlement Administration at the U.S. Department of Agriculture, naming Columbia University economics professor Rexford Guy Tugwell as director. Even before authorization, Tugwell had enlisted John Lansill and his staff of planners from Agriculture's Land Utilization Division to begin creating new towns that combined elements of both urban and rural social welfare programs.

The previous year, Roosevelt had directed agriculture secretary Henry Wallace to develop a homestead program for subsistence farming, but progress was slow, and the program had virtually no national impact. Farmers were in desperate straits—cotton was 5.5 cents a pound, down from a 1909–14 average of 14.5 cents; wheat was 32.3 cents a bushel, down from 88.4 cents—and there was no point in moving the urban poor to the countryside without also providing work, food, and shelter. Life on the farm was also considered undesirable, even by most farmers. The headline of the July 17, 1935, edition of *Variety*, "Hicks Nix Sticks Pix," suggested that even rural audiences did not like rural plots and characters in movies. Recognizing the same set of problems as Wright, federal officials developed a mixed-use plan, incorporating industrial and agricultural job opportunities with new housing under the banner of the Suburban Division of the Resettlement Administration. John Lansill, a patrician from Lexington, Kentucky, and a Tugwell protégé, led the effort. The competition for funding was fierce, with Harold Ickes and Harry Hopkins at the Public Works Administration fighting a pitched battle with Tugwell and each other for money appropriated by Congress for emergency relief.

Tugwell emerged in the spring of 1935 with $30 million of the $68 million he had sought. With virtually no time to plan—Congress and the White House demanded immediate results—Lansill moved into spectacularly inappropriate office space, a rococo 54-room mansion at 2020 Massachusetts Avenue, N.W., in Washington, a gift made by the heiress Evalyn Walsh McLean. Lansill's design team moved desks into madame's boudoir and bathroom and began to develop a site near Highstown (now Roosevelt), New Jersey, breaking ground less than a hundred days after Roosevelt signed the executive order creating the program. The result, Jersey Homesteads, represented a successful political effort by the White House. It drew David Dubinsky, president of the International Ladies Garment Workers Union, away from Norman Thomas and the Socialist Party into the New Deal coalition, an effort to invade political party lines as the Democrats picked up steam heading into the 1936 election. The plan for Jersey Homesteads was the resettlement of 200 Jewish families from New York's Lower East Side, all of whom had worked in the garment industry. An additional 25 families were selected to operate other businesses necessary to the settlement. Highstown provided housing, a factory for making dresses (at union wages), a grocery store, and a dairy and poultry farm, all cooperatively owned. Each family invested $500 and was given a house on an acre of land and long-term credit to pay back the $1 million cost of the project (about $4,200 per family). The houses were ample, five- and six-room Georgian-style bungalows, accompanied by an uncompromising Bauhaus community building designed by Alfred Kastner and graced with a Ben Shahn mural. The construction manager of Highstown, Max Blitzer, told a reporter, "We hope to prove that the benefits of semi-rural life carried out on a cooperative community basis will materially raise the standard of living of garment workers." Given the complexity of issues, competing interests, and red tape, it is a wonder that anything was built.

In Tugwell's mind neither Highstown, designed for urban factory workers, nor Norris Village in Tennessee, designed for rural families who worked for TVA, achieved the synthesis of urban-rural advantages that would reverse the cycles of unemployment and poverty in both city and countryside. A program that he first called "rurban housing" developed into the greenbelt town program, a scheme loosely based on the Ebenezer Howard–Raymond Unwin plans in Great Britain. With greenbelt towns, Tugwell hoped to provide work relief in construction projects—building the town itself—which in turn would combine decent housing, community planning, and subsistence farming. With time and money at a premium, only four sites were selected from an original nine, and only three were eventually built: Greenbelt, Maryland, outside Washington, D. C.; Greenhills, Ohio, near Cincinnati; and Greendale, Wisconsin, in the Milwaukee suburbs. By summer 1935, the plan was in trouble, and several members of the Regional Planning Association of America in New York were asked to come in and rescue the project. Clarence Stein, Henry Wright, Stuart Chase, Catherine Bauer, and others were hired as consultants. From TVA, the chief of town planning (and another RPAA member), Tracy Augur, was also recruited, and he in turn enlisted Roland Wank, TVA's chief architect, to supervise design at Greenhills, with John Nolen, Sr., doing the planning.

The organizing principle behind the greenbelt towns was the superblock, which provided parklike settings for housing with a separation between motor and foot traffic in a scheme similar to Henry Wright's layout at Radburn, New Jersey, of 1929, and Chatham Village in Pittsburgh, of 1932. Years later Mumford claimed that "had it not been for the ideas that the Regional Planning Association of America under Stein's presidency had put into circulation during the twenties, the Greenbelt Towns undertaken by the Resettlement Administration in 1934 would have been inconceivable...."

Wright was well represented at the Resettlement Administration, where former Taliesin apprentices Phil Holliday, Jim Drought, Lewis Stevens, Harry Yardley, Sam Ratensky, and Joe Kastner all worked. Drought, a planner who worked for Lansill, had known Frederick Gutheim at the Experimental College after working for Wright briefly a year before the Fellowship began. He later returned to Wisconsin to work on the Greendale project. Holliday, a graphic designer, had helped Wright put together the first brochures on the Fellowship. Lewis Stevens and Sam Ratensky were both charter apprentices.

Highstown was a far cry from Broadacre City. New Deal experimentation, whether TVA or at the Resettlement Administration, was the purview of economists and sociologists, not architects. Roosevelt wanted projects that would gain national attention as demonstrations of the next wave in the fight for recovery of the nation's economic health, and Washington was a bear market for new solutions that could have an immediate impact. Wright needed work. As he began to discover the realities of Washington, his rhetoric shifted somewhat from physical to social planning, from roads to economics. When the Broadacre City exhibit opened at the Corcoran Gallery in Washington on July 2, 1935, he invited John Lansill. Two long pieces in *The Washington Post* had already paved the road to Broadacre City for Roosevelt officials. In the Sunday before the Tuesday exhibit opening, the *Post* reporter enthusiastically suggested that New Deal experts had something to learn from Wright:

> In a day when New Deal specialists are struggling with resettlement projects, housing ideas and community planning on an important scale, nothing could be more pertinent than to study the suggestions of this architectural giant as exemplified in his miniature "ideal community."

Two days later, Wright was interviewed in a follow-up piece. "I have not invented," he said, paying some allegiance to government planners, "but I do believe I have the capacity to interpret, else I wouldn't have the courage to look myself in the face when anyone calls me an architect."

The next day, Wright met with Lansill beneath a ceiling painting of pink cherubs that encircled a chandelier in Evalyn McLean's boudoir. Wright immediately got to the point, suggesting that the Resettlement Administration abandon its greenbelt towns, find another $70 million to add to the $30 million already appropriated and permit him to build "the finest city in the world," stipulating that it must be handled by him with "no interference" from the government. According to Lansill, "Had Wright been willing to work within the liberal guidelines imposed on the rest of the planning teams, the Resettlement Administration would have considered Broadacre City." When Lansill explained the conditions under which Broadacre City would be considered, Wright denounced "all public and private housing in America and never again communicated with the Suburban Division."

144

(Opposite) Living and dining areas, Rosenbaum house, Florence, Alabama. Note similarities with the perspective renderings for the Hoult and Lusk houses (see page 138).

8. THE USONIANS

As the Broadacre City model began its tour and the Fellowship returned to Spring Green, life at Taliesin changed. With publicity generated by the exhibit and lectures, and the greater visibility of the Fellowship, important commissions began to come Wright's way. Edgar Kaufmann, Jr.'s, tenure with the Fellowship led to jobs from Edgar senior: first the Broadacre models, then Fallingwater, the Kaufmanns' retreat at Bear Run off the Youghiogheny River in Pennsylvania. These were followed by the S. C. Johnson Administration building; Wingspread, the Herbert Johnson residence at Racine, Wisconsin; and the Hanna house in Palo Alto, California. All of these projects drew on architectural ideas that had been percolating for some time; all were grandly conceived and meticulously executed; all helped to renew Wright's celebrity as a working professional, not simply the teacher and theoretician he feared he had become.

Now that the wealthy Kaufmanns of Pennsylvania and Johnsons of Wisconsin had confidence to build with Wright, clients with limited resources were given courage to consider the unthinkable—a Frank Lloyd Wright house of their own. But in the first round of the Wright renaissance, clients still came mostly from the friends and neighbors of Taliesin. One exception was the Hannas, who first contacted Wright after reading his published Kahn lectures. Paul and Jean Hanna were invited to Taliesin and paid Wright a visit on the way to Minnesota, where they had both been born and bred. Like Wright's father and grandfather and his Uncle Jenkin, both the Hannas' fathers were Protestant ministers. The Hannas' backgrounds were also similar to the Willeys'. Both couples were intellectuals, committed to their families and to Wright's ideas. Both were Deweyites. Both had nest eggs and lived comfortably, but were not wealthy, although the Hannas were somewhat better off than the Willeys. When the Hannas first approached Wright, they proposed building a house in The Bronx, on land owned by Columbia University, where they both taught. Later, when the Columbia arrangement fell through and they had moved to California, they made a similar proposal to Stanford University, leasing a hillside site for $100 a year.

But the Hanna house, completed in 1937, cost $37,000, too large and too expensive to advance solutions to the problem of creating a low-cost house. Soon enough, the opportunity came from journalist Herbert Jacobs and his wife Katherine, whose artist cousin, Harold Wescott, had been at Taliesin for a summer and arranged their first appointment after Herbert had interviewed Wright for his newspaper. Once again, a minister's son found inspiration in Wright's work. Herbert Austin Jacobs was born in Milwaukee in 1900. He grew up in his father's south side parish, a settlement house called the Wisconsin University Settlement Association, a center for social action in the spirit of Hull House with close ties to the University of Wisconsin in Madison. At the end of World War I Jacobs entered Harvard on a scholarship, ascending to an editorship of the *Crimson* by his senior year. Incredibly, he turned down a Rhodes fellowship, declaring to his friends that he did not want to become a perpetual student. Instead, he returned to Wisconsin, became a cub reporter on the staff of the *Milwaukee Journal*, and moved on in 1934 to the *Capital Times* in Madison, where he earned $38 a week and rolled his own cigarettes to save money. Jacobs served as the president of the Newspaper Guild, the journalists' union, at both papers. In Madison Jacobs came into daily contact with university intellectuals and statehouse progressives, including Alexander Meikeljohn, David Lilienthal, John Kenneth Galbraith, Philip La Follette, and Frank and Olgivanna Wright and their band of apprentices.

In addition to their idealism and devotion to the Wrights' way of life, the Jacobses were practical folks, ready to sacrifice and trade their own toil for a piece of Taliesin on their land in Westmorland, a Madison development of small houses. Katherine was drawn to Wright as a character who combined qualities of her father and her husband. She had been raised on a dairy farm near West Bend, Wisconsin, the youngest of six children of a hard-working couple who lost their land and stock to the Depression. The family moved to Ripon, where her father got a job with the Farm Bureau and Katherine went to Ripon College while living at home, then moved to Milwaukee, where she finally landed a job—$5 a week, room and board—as a bookstore clerk. Soon afterward she met Herbert Jacobs and first heard of Frank Lloyd Wright, whose new autobiography was the talk of Milwaukee. "The customers weren't interested in architecture," remembered Katherine, "but all those east side fancy women wanted all the gory stories of his life."

At their first encounter with Wright as a couple, Herbert bravely offered that "what this country needs is a good $5,000 house," understanding from his previous interview that it was a problem of great interest to Wright. "Do you want a $5,000 house," Wright replied, "or a $10,000 house for $5,000?" Soon enough the Jacobses were working with Wright. The six-foot-one Herbert had only one firm request of the design: a higher ceiling. "I want to be able to wear my hat anywhere in the house, including the bedroom," he told Wright.

The Jacobs house was contracted at a fixed price that was guaranteed by the Taliesin Fellowship, an unusual arrangement that Wright did not repeat. But as an experiment the house worked beautifully. A contract was let to a contractor enthusiastic to build with Wright, and the project stayed close to budget with the free assistance of Taliesin apprentices, Herbert and Katherine's constant help, and Taliesin-appropriated materials from the Racine site of the S. C. Johnson Administration building, which was under construction

House for Herbert and Katherine Jacobs, 441 Toepfer Street, Westmorland, Wisconsin, near Madison, 1936–37

at the time. The house was completed in 1937 at a final cost of $5,500, but the experiment was never replicated on another site.

The Jacobs house was a culmination of Wright's efforts to simplify plan, structure, materials, and hardware into a dwelling that middle-income families could afford, but that combined the warmth and charm of his larger houses with the functionality necessary for a modern family. The approach and entry are covered by a carport, a simple extension of a flat roof that continues in a straight line over the two bedrooms, and a woodworking shop and study. At right angles is a higher roof, also flat, over the living room, dining area, and kitchen work space. This arrangement of family spaces—at right angles to individual spaces—provides a great sense of separation within a relatively small space. Indeed, the Jacobs house seems much larger than its actual square footage, a consequence of the varied ceiling heights, of continuous fenestration in the living room and prospects to outdoors throughout the house, and of the use of built-in furniture and cabinetry to leave much of the floor space uncluttered.

Another contribution to the feeling of spaciousness is the visible two-by-four-foot module, a grid that is etched into the concrete floor and the fiberboard ceiling, revealing the architect's intentions while acting as a unifying element of the design. This grid also complements the horizontal transom windows, the board-and-batten wall units, and masonry with the mortar brick-colored in the vertical joints and white and recessed in the horizontal joints, a reference to the module that also contributes to the long, low profile of the house on its site. The Jacobs house was potentially a system—a kit of parts—that could be configured in an infinite number of ways to suit the needs of a particular site and client.

As the house neared completion, Jacobs's rival newspaper, the *Wisconsin State Journal,* scooped his *Capital Times* with a front-page story on Wright's "new $5,500 house," which was put on the news wire and distributed to newspapers coast to coast. Trumpeted across America as an answer to the need for low-cost housing, the Jacobs house achieved instant celebrity, flooding Taliesin with inquiries from prospective clients.

Wright's fortunes began to improve. In 1938 Henry Luce offered him a grand slam at national recognition. The entire 102-page editorial section of the January *Architectural Forum* was by and about Wright, while at *Time,* a cover story, "Usonian Architect," reached the nearly million readers of its January 17 issue, presenting Wright as "gracious, mischievous and immaculate at 68," a "worthy peer" of Thoreau and Whitman. Later that year, *Life,* with more than three million in circulation, published renderings and plans for eight small houses—four modern and four in traditional styles, for families with incomes of $2,000–$10,000 a year—including a new Usonian house designed by Frank Lloyd Wright. The architects were asked to design for a particular family's needs, and Wright was given Minneapolis publisher Albert R. Blackbourne, his wife, and two teenage children as clients. Wright designed what he called "A Private Little Club," a four-bedroom house with an open, 60-foot living room and a dining alcove. "Space," according to Wright, "is characteristic of this free pattern for a freer life than you could possibly live in the conventional house." The Blackbournes selected a traditional house anyway, but Wright's house was built the following year for another client, Bernard Schwartz, in Two Rivers, Wisconsin.

During that year Wright received commissions to design 27 houses from clients living in the West (California and Arizona); the Midwest (Ohio, Michigan, Illinois, and Wisconsin); and the South (Virginia, South

Carolina, Alabama, and Florida). Of the 27, a dozen were built. Wright began to develop the Usonian house as a kit of parts, later classified by John Sergeant according to layout: Polliwog or "L" (the Jacobs plan), Diagonal, Hexagonal, In-line, and Raised Usonian. Of the 12 houses built in 1939, seven were Usonians: the Rosenbaum house in Alabama, a house for Katherine Winckler and Alma Goetsch, residences for the Bazett

family and Bernard Sturges in California, the Pope house in Virginia, the Euchtman house in Maryland, and the Sondern house in Kansas City. The Aztec-inspired Pauson house in Arizona, while having a Usonian plan, was too severely regional to be considered in the same vein as the other houses that were designed that year. The other five houses of 1939, such as the Lloyd Lewis house in Illinois and Auldbrass Plantation in Yemassee, South Carolina, were organic houses that did not fit the modest specifications of the Usonian.

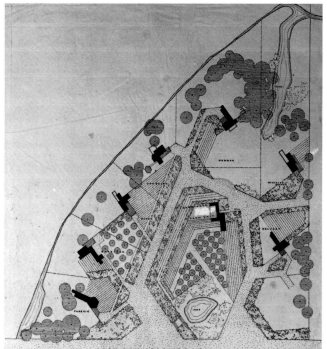

Site plan for Usonia 2, 1939. The Winckler-Goetsch residence, included in the plan, was built in Okemos, Michigan, after banks refused financing for Usonia 2. Another house in the plan, for Erling Brauner (1948), was later revised and built in Okemos, with the substitution of textile block for cypress board and batten walls.

Following the Jacobs model, the first follow-up generic Usonians using the Polliwog layout and the standard Usonian details that had been developed in 1938 were single story and of moderate cost and could be built on any relatively flat lot. These included the Rosenbaum and Pope houses and a larger version for J. J. Garrison, one of the houses in an ensemble confusingly called Usonia 2, designed for a group of seven faculty families at Michigan State University in Lansing.

The Rosenbaum house, in Florence, Alabama, was far from the city, attuned to its site and locale, fundamentals of Wright's ideas for Usonia. Elizabeth Kassler, a 1932 charter apprentice at Taliesin and a curator of architecture at the Museum of Modern Art from 1938 to 1946, remembered the house as "the best of the Usonians." John Sergeant, in *Frank Lloyd Wright's Usonian Houses*, describes it as "The purest example of the Usonian, …combin[ing] all the standard elements in a mature and spatially varied interior." Like many other Wright clients, the Rosenbaums were drawn to Frank Lloyd Wright for reasons that stretched beyond the design of his houses, a sensibility that captured the spirit of a culture that ran at right angles to mainstream tastes.

The Rosenbaum family had moved to Florence twenty years earlier. Louis Rosenbaum had been an immigrant who had fled Lublin, in eastern Poland, arriving with his mother and younger brother in America in the summer of 1893. After trying various occupations he had become a movie theater owner in Douglas, Wyoming, and in 1918 he selected the boom town of Florence to build a new movie palace, the Princess Theater, complete with red velvet seats, a gold proscenium, a huge chandelier, an orchestra pit, and a mighty Wurlitzer organ. In spite of the defeat of Henry Ford's proposal for Muscle Shoals, Rosenbaum had expanded his entertainment business. By 1927 he had added the Ritz and the Palace in Sheffield and the Strand in Tuscumbia to the Princess and Majestic theaters in Florence. His son Stanley entered Harvard in 1927 and graduated with honors in 1931. Stanley's search for a college teaching job was made difficult by the Depression and impossible by lingering anti-Semitism in departments of arts and letters of most academic institutions. Without a prospect by the close of the summer, he traveled to Colorado to live with an uncle and attend the University of Denver, where he received a master's degree in 1932.

After he returned to Florence, he settled into a job with his father, managing the Ritz Theater in Sheffield, which left enough spare time to edit a local literary magazine and to feed his insatiable appetite for anything in print. Over Louis's office at the Princess, 15-year-old Aaron Green, a talented cartoonist and artist, painted signs for the theaters, an after-school job that continued into his college years. Several years later, as an architecture student at Cooper Union in New York, Green would persuade Stanley Rosenbaum and his bride to build with Frank Lloyd Wright, after which Green joined the Taliesin Fellowship. His relationship with Wright and Taliesin evolved over the next four decades, as apprentice, staff member, and sometime partner.

Louis Rosenbaum's first theater in Florence, the Princess, shown here c.1937

Muscle Shoals had not been hit as hard by the stock market crash as some other places. Its main bank, while not thriving, was solvent. Local businesses were generally not tied to big concerns, except for farmers, who suffered terribly when the price of cotton descended to almost nothing. Still, nearly everyone went to the movies at least once a week. Like the Model T, motion pictures had become a staple of modern life, a near necessity, one of the few industries in America that prospered during those years. Stanley Rosenbaum struck a balance, taking an active part in Florence life, but also escaping into books and movies and traveling once or twice a year to New York to see friends and Broadway shows and to troll the shelves of the Gotham Book Mart, which displayed a sign in its window, "Wise Men Fish Here." It was not until he planned to build with Wright in 1939 that Stanley read Frank Lloyd Wright's *Autobiography*, although he probably raised an eyebrow when he read Shelton Cheney's 1932 review of it in the *Saturday Review of Literature*, which called it "one of the most trenchant and most beautiful books of our time."

Stanley's interest in the arts lay first in English literature and poetry, but he did read all the important popular American writers, ordering books by mail as their reviews appeared, including Sinclair Lewis, Pearl Buck, Booth Tarkington, Thornton Wilder, and Ernest Hemingway. In the other arts, his taste was eclectic. The movies formed his ideas of design through the Art Deco aesthetic of the 1930s—glamorous New York apartments and nightclubs, the urban fantasies of Hugh Ferriss. Outside the Princess, in the daylight of Florence's residential streets, the style was bland, strings of bungalows punctuated by a few gingerbread Gothics and a few mansions in classical modes, with Doric porticos obscured by huge, spreading magnolias. Florence was southern in culture, but its residential streets could have been in Xenia, Ohio, or Paducah, Kentucky, for dreams of young Florence families of a home of their own looked just like the dreams of others who lived in the towns of middle America. The style of its small houses—the English cottage in all its variations—was the standard for the middle landscape between city and country from the Chesapeake Bay to the Great Plains and from the Great Lakes to the Tennessee Valley. Without being native or regional, these all-American houses gave comfort, providing a link to the ancestral roots of most of the population. In Florence, almost everyone came from Scots-Irish forebears, who settled the area between the time when the last Creek and Cherokee Indians left and the first blue-coated soldiers arrived.

For newer American settlers, particularly those who had been oppressed by tyrants, free expression, free elections, economic opportunity, and access to a university education were the pillars of a new life. Frank Lloyd Wright's architecture gave form to those ideas and aspirations for those who looked beyond their ancestry or locale to something uniquely American, its variations determined by the characteristics of its site and its occupants, not by conformity with its neighbors. While Stanley Rosenbaum was a hometown boy, he had gone away to Harvard, was the son of immigrants and a member of a religious minority, and worked in a business that was spun from fantasies. His life in Florence was enviable, yet set apart, with one foot in and one foot out. Like other immigrant families, Stanley's demonstrated their appreciation of a new culture by identifying with the makers of modern America, such as Franklin Roosevelt and Frank Lloyd Wright.

In 1938 Stanley married Mildred (Mimi) Bookholtz, whom he had met on one of his trips to New York. After graduating from high school in The Bronx, she had gone to work as a model for the John Robert Powers Agency while attending Hunter College at night. In an economics class, she had been assigned a paper on the Tennessee Valley Authority. "I worked harder on that paper than anything else," she recalled. Three years later, when Mimi married Stanley Rosenbaum and moved to Florence—at the heart of TVA—it was exciting, like "going off to a kibbutz in Israel, only better." Her mother had encouraged her. "Gussie Bookholtz was a socialist, although she loved Eleanor Roosevelt, who had said that 'TVA would put shoes on the poor children's feet,'" Mimi recalled. As a wedding present from Stanley's parents, Stanley and Mimi were presented with a large building lot and a check for $7,500 to build their dream house, directly across the street from Louis and Anna Rosenbaum's house on Riverview Drive.

The newlyweds selected Stanley's friend Aaron Green as their architect; but after struggling with various problems, Green suggested that they abandon his preliminary design and engage Frank Lloyd Wright. "But I'm sure that Wright is too expensive," Rosenbaum protested. "Let's ask him," replied Green. He wrote to Wright the following day:

Stanley Rosenbaum and Mildred Bookholtz on Riverside Drive, New York, 1938

April 20, 1939
427 E. Mobile Street
Florence, Alabama

Frank Lloyd Wright
Taliesin, Wisconsin

Dear Sir:

As a student of architecture, an enthusiastic admirer of your work, and a student of yours, even if indirectly, this opportunity to write is considered a privilege. However, it is not to deviate into a "fan" letter.

Bids for a house which I have designed were excessive. Rather than begin again or destroy the unity of the house by the usual methods of cutting, I suggested to the client, optimistically, that you be asked to design the house. Because, as well as clients, the people are my friends, and because your solution would be far superior to another's attempt in applying your ideas and philosophy, I would very much prefer your personal solution.

The client which I offer you will be happy to leave all considerations of the building in your hands. They are familiar with your ideas and achievements through your published works, which I possess and prize. They have absorbed my interpretations of some and are now quite as enthusiastic as I.

The couple are recently married, the young man a Harvard graduate, writer, and poet. Both should be capable of bearing children deserving of your "Usonian" house. Acquainted with your Jacobs house, I am well aware of your ability to cope with a similar situation.

The existing obstacle is a maximum of $7500.00. The client is willing that you do the job "cost plus" or bids may be submitted for contract. The family requires a three bedroom house with study. The plot, 124 x 140 feet, slopes to the south, and faces a broad uninterrupted view of the Tennessee river on the exposure.

This section of the country, without a doubt, presents as backward an architectural expression as can be possible. This despite the fact that it is immediately in the midst of the T.V.A. engineering developments, and a part of the Muscle Shoals district. We need a local architecture.

I realize that the amount involved is very small, but the idea presented itself partly because I thought this section of the country would interest you, and because I understand that you are at the present time working on a Florida school project [Florida Southern College]. This should be near your route of travel.

My official architectural training has been received at Cooper Union, N.Y.C. and at present I am debating the advisability of returning in October for a finishing year. A close study of your published works has resulted in far more actual benefit. If for nothing more than the experience of a visit through your recent house in Great Neck L.I. [Rebhuhn residence, completed in 1938], I sincerely thank you.

Your early reply regarding the contents of this letter will be greatly appreciated.

Sincerely,
A. G. Green

Green's letter was worded to appeal to Wright in its description of the clients, the site, the location, and the broader architectural opportunity the project presented, as well as in the offer of his own availability as a apprentice; by then, Wright had discovered that on-site supervision by one of his own was vital to the success of any project.

Full of expectation, Green sent the letter; then three long months passed without word from Wright, who had left the Fellowship in Arizona only a few days before Green mailed his letter to deliver a series of lectures to the Royal Institute of British Architects in London. The letter was addressed to Wisconsin, where it remained unopened until the Fellowship returned from the West and the Wrights from London. In addition, Taliesin was by then flooded with work, with more than 20 projects on the boards or under construction. Finally, on July 26, they heard from Wright by letter from Spring Green, saying only: "My dear Green: Will be glad to go through with a house for your clients. Perhaps you can follow through, with our assistance, in the execution."

The Rosenbaums were delighted, and Green responded a few days later with more details, writing, "A rather unusual circumstance exists. The parents of the young clients have their home directly across the street. You will notice in the drawing, a division line, 32 feet from the lot line. This space is to be kept free of building which would obstruct the view of those across the street, although the space will be included in the landscaping." About two weeks later, Stanley Rosenbaum wrote directly to Wright, providing additional details of their needs. Awaiting word from Wright, Green was wondering if he should stay in Florence or return to New York. "In no attempt to rush you," the 22-year-old Green cautiously wrote to the 72-year-old Wright, "but with avid enthusiasm and interest, we write again...to inquire of the house. Expecting to hear from you before this, we are now in a state of...well, wondering."

Meanwhile, war broke out in Europe. Four days after England and France declared war on Germany, another letter came for Green from Gene Masselink, noting that no mention had been made of Wright's fee, which was 10 percent of the total cost of the house, one indication of the improved fortunes of Taliesin. Without yet receiving Green's reply regarding his fee, Wright had already completed a set of preliminary drawings and sent them to the Rosenbaums, with a note saying, "I intended the sketches to be sent to you but by mistake here they went directly to Rosenbaum. I hope you all like them. A nice house to live in down there?"

Stanley Rosenbaum replied immediately upon receiving the plans, respectfully making a few suggestions, but clearly pleased with the design. A few days later, Wright thanked Rosenbaum for his check, promising to take care of the suggested changes. On the same day Wright also wrote to Green, noting that the usual methods of contracting for construction did not work very well in the construction of one of his houses. "We itemize all mill work—let contracts for piece work—brick per thousand laid and measured in a wall—concrete per cu-ft laid, lumber according to our bill, etc. etc." Wright went on to explain that "this throws a whole strain on us incommensurate with an architect's fee and we meet it by sending on an apprentice at the proper time to take charge, do shopping and hold the whole together...." He asked the Rosenbaums to lodge and feed the apprentice, cover his travel expenses, and pay the Fellowship $25 per week for his services "so long as required (it should not be in this case longer than ten weeks)." Wright also explained, "We have standardized details during the years we have been working on the modest priced house problem and feel that in this way we can not only save our clients most of the general contractor's fee but get results of which we can be proud."

With no word for more than a month, Green wrote to Wright on October 21: "We are having fine building weather here now. Please let us know when to expect your man and the working drawings." Masselink responded to Green immediately that they were in the mail. "Mr. Wright suggests you can do a little preliminary skirmishing until our man can get down to you." With the plans came a set of specifications, and Green set to work locating men and materials for the job. The Rosenbaums set two conditions that made his job of holding down costs impossible. The first was their insistence on using only local suppliers for materials. Green complained to Wright, "The scope of [my] scouting has been somewhat limited by Rosenbaum's desire to confine his purchase of materials to our local dealers, of which there are only three, all holding to practically the same price standard." The second condition was that the project employ only union labor.

Finally, after New Year's Day, with the arrival of Wright's apprentice, Burt Goodrich, work started. Goodrich wrote to Wright that the bids were very high as "Mr. R. Senior [Louis Rosenbaum] wants to use union labor and to patronize his local friends if possible." But by fits and starts, with cost overruns, through bad weather and a series of minor disasters, the house that Wright designed for the Rosenbaums was built,

USONIA HOUSE FOR MILDRED and STANLEY ROSENBAUM
FLORENCE ALABAMA

Perspective drawing of the southern facade of the Rosenbaums' Usonian house, Florence, Alabama, dated September 10, 1939. On the left between the trees, Wright sketched in a conventional dwelling across the street, complying with Aaron Green's request to leave Louis Rosenbaum's view of the river unobstructed.

Rosenbaum house under construction, February 1940

with Burt Goodrich and Aaron Green virtually living on the site from January to August. Goodrich's 10 weeks stretched to 35.

No one on the site had any experience in building a Frank Lloyd Wright house. It was a first house for both Green and Goodrich. After the concrete mat was poured and the masonry masses were set into place, Goodrich tried to traverse the space between piers with wood beams, a span of 30 feet across the living room. The previous year Edgar Tafel and Wes Peters had discovered the same problem in the drawings for the two-story Schwartz house with its 30-foot living room and had quietly added steel beams without telling Wright. In his book, Tafel explained:

When [Goodrich] went south—soon after this—to supervise a similar house, Wes and I took him aside and gave him the facts of structural life, "Tuck the steel away thusly and nobody will know...." The apprentice was chicken; he followed the original plans. When the props came down, so did the roof. [Stanley Rosenbaum] called Mr. Wright, whose response was "Send the boy back to Taliesin." Returning to the fold would solve everything. Mr. Wright had the plans brought out and inspected the structure. I admitted adding steel to the Schwartz house. "I can deal with my enemies, but cannot trust my own apprentices.... You have violated my trust.... This is the end."

After Olgivanna Wright intervened, Tafel was re-instated, and steel was added to the Rosenbaums' specifications. Soon afterward Stanley called Wright again, complaining that the doorways to the bed-rooms and bathrooms were too narrow. Wright replied that he had made them 20 inches, which was several inches wider than the doors to compart-ments in a Pullman car. "I never heard of anyone getting stuck on a train," he told Stanley, who was not very reassured.

In mid-July, Stanley wrote to his college friend Julian Altman in Chicago, "...Strange as it seems, we're not yet living in the Frank Lloyd Wright house, though we hope to be doing so by August first. We've had lots of trouble. The difficulty in building a revolutionary house is that every detail becomes a

Rosenbaum house under construction, July 1940

special problem, since all hardware, etc., is made to fit traditional houses. It's cost me more than I figured, too, and it looks like I'll be in debt for years. But nevertheless the house itself is extremely satisfactory and we are very much sold on Wright." Rosenbaum continued, "...The house has made a sensation in Florence. I believe every one in town has been to see it at least three times. We have had not less than 100 visitors a day on week-days for the past few months, and the number runs as high as 500 on Saturdays."

Finally, on August 23, Rosenbaum informed Wright, "The house is completed and we are living in it.... [It] is absolutely breathtaking. Aesthetically, I don't believe any of your other houses will rank higher. We have tried to be absolutely consistent in the furnishing. Burt designed the smaller pieces of furniture to supplement those which you designed for us. It was all specially made—down to the waste-baskets and trays.

Rosenbaum house, from the south, September 1940. Photograph by G. E. Kidder Smith.

The only piece of furniture in the house which is an exception is the Baldwin grand piano." The house followed the Jacobs house plan and grid but had more space and more refined details, in keeping with a larger lot and budget.

As the Rosenbaums moved into their new residence, they received a letter from the Museum of Modern Art, requesting information on the house, followed by a request to send G. E. Kidder Smith to Florence to make photographs in September. Within a few weeks after they moved in, photographs of the Rosenbaums' new house were on display in New York as part of MoMA's large Frank Lloyd Wright exhibition. The house complete, Aaron Green left Florence with Burt Goodrich to make his life at Taliesin, first working on the MoMA exhibition. Within a year he was supervising Cooperative Homesteads, a Resettlement Administration–inspired development of berm houses for Ford workers in Royal Oak, Michigan, a project conceived in part by Morris Mitchell, a progressive visionary who was a friend of the Rosenbaums and Green in Florence, where he taught at the local college. In the end the project was canceled when the Ford workers were transformed into draftees after Pearl Harbor. After the war Green settled in California, where he collaborated with Wright and Taliesin on a number of projects, including supervision of the Marin

Rosenbaum house living room, September 1940. Photograph by G. E. Kidder Smith

County Center, one of the largest of the Wright building ensembles. Eventually Green became perhaps the closest of Wright's protégés, the only member of Wright's staff to operate a Wright office outside of the two Taliesins, in San Francisco's Chinatown.

In 1947, with three children and a fourth on the way, Stanley and Mimi Rosenbaum would visit Wright in Spring Green to discuss an addition to the house. The weekend of their visit Ayn Rand was also expected, to talk to Wright about sets for the movie based on her novel *The Fountainhead*, whose chief character, the architect Howard Roark, was modeled on Wright. She had written in the visual instructions of her screenplay, "Among present day architects, it is the style of Frank Lloyd Wright—and only of Frank Lloyd Wright—that must be taken as a model for Roark's buildings." By dinnertime on Sunday she had not arrived. Wright, as usual, was late. While they waited at the dinner table with other guests and with Wes Peters and Olgivanna Wright, Stanley Rosenbaum remarked that he had just read a new book by the historian Arnold Toynbee, who had named Frank Lloyd Wright the greatest architect since the Renaissance. It was the most flattering thing he could think of to say. After a pause Olgivanna Wright turned to Rosenbaum and Peters. "And who do you suppose Professor Toynbee was talking about in the Renaissance? Was it Brunelleschi? Alberti? Perhaps Palladio?" Stanley said nothing, letting others at the table speculate as to which Renaissance architect was greater than the master, Frank Lloyd Wright.

■

With the Usonian house Wright was pursuing two ideas that characterized successful innovation in American design: the development of a prototype that could be applied universally and the invention of a kit of parts that could be infinitely reconfigured. Like the Model T, the Usonian house was designed to be centrally manufactured and shipped in pieces to be assembled on site, as the car was assembled at regional depots. The early Usonians also aspired to meet another test of American success: the establishment of a widely recognized brand name and widespread, favorable publicity.

Each of Wright's early efforts not only addressed the problem of providing a sensible house for middle-income families, but also can be viewed as part of the strategy for Broadacre City, combining demonstration of the kit and a method of distribution: matching projects to clients across the country, and gaining publicity for the Usonian house and its new name. The Rosenbaum house was in the heart of TVA, the most prominent and promising showcase of the New Deal. The Pope house was built in a near-suburb of Washington, D.C., at a time when Greenbelt, Maryland, also outside Washington, was under construction and the subject of extensive press attention. The client, Loren Pope, wrote for the *Washington Star*. Wright had already gained significant additional exposure from Herbert Jacobs, another journalist who had written about his house after it was completed. The Museum of Modern Art Usonian prototype would obviously have gained considerable attention, at least as much publicity as the Broadacre City exhibit five years earlier. The Florida and Michigan projects were also designed as part of a site plan, fragments of Broadacre City being tested on the landscape. The next two houses of the series, both in-line Usonians (rather than on an L), continued the pattern of model and kit: the Winckler-Goetsch house, designed as one of the Lansing group (and later built in Okemos, Michigan), and the Euchtman house in Baltimore, near Washington.

Wright's publicity efforts did not always work. Of the Museum of Modern Art show, Geoffrey Baker, writing in the *New York Times*, asked, "Why not more emphasis on earlier work?" The Wright exhibit was hung in tandem with a film retrospective of D. W. Griffith, another indication that Wright was mainly considered in the past tense—"half-modern," as Philip Johnson said in 1932. The *Times* critic dismissed Usonian houses as impractical, giving rise to a rebuttal from Herbert Jacobs the following week and further comment from Baker. "No one is more eager that I to see an improvement in the design of the $5,000-and-under house. In this Wright certainly has some contributions to make, possibly by inspiration rather than example." But he concluded that "unconventional design and methods [were] likely to cost more" by creating problems for FHA financing.

His conclusion had some basis in fact. The Willeys and Hannas were able to build their houses with Wright because of their secure university appointments and family savings. The Hoults and the Lusks were more conservative in their tastes, and perhaps more dependent on federally guaranteed bank financing, which was not approved. The Jacobs house was financed by a local mortgage lender—a Wright devotee since a childhood visit to Midway Gardens—after the FHA had rejected their application. By 1939 virtually all of Wright's houses were funded through either family savings or private financing. The Rosenbaums paid for their house through a gift and loan from Stanley Rosenbaum's father. Others found alternative means, like Loren Pope, who obtained a mortgage for his house through the *Washington Star*, his employer.

In sum, special circumstances and a degree of risk-taking were necessary to build with Wright. Herbert Jacobs and Stanley Rosenbaum, both Harvard-educated intellectuals, were drawn to Wright by their idealism, qualities that the more business-minded Charles Hoult and Robert Lusk may not have had to the same degree. Apart from FHA regulations, the Jacobses and Rosenbaums moved from idea to execution without a backward glance, while the Hoults and Lusks were demonstably less determined.

More than ever Wright's work in the mid-to-late 1930s was motivated by his desire for recognition and influence across the whole of American architecture, a fight against the European sterility of the Bauhaus, which was beginning to dominate the sensibility of the nation's architects and schools of architecture. Wright's energies were directed toward large signature projects such as the S. C. Johnson and Son Administration Building and the Herbert Johnson residence, Fallingwater, the Guggenheim Museum (with the first design completed in 1943), and Taliesin West; a solution to the small house problem; and the Broadacre town plan. As Wright's fame and reputation grew, generating an increasing number of commissions, and as the first members of the Fellowship developed experience to assume greater responsibility over the work in the office (part of the strategy to provide distribution for Usonian houses), Wright was increasingly able to focus his attention on these three interlocking areas of work, a focus that continued until his death in 1959.

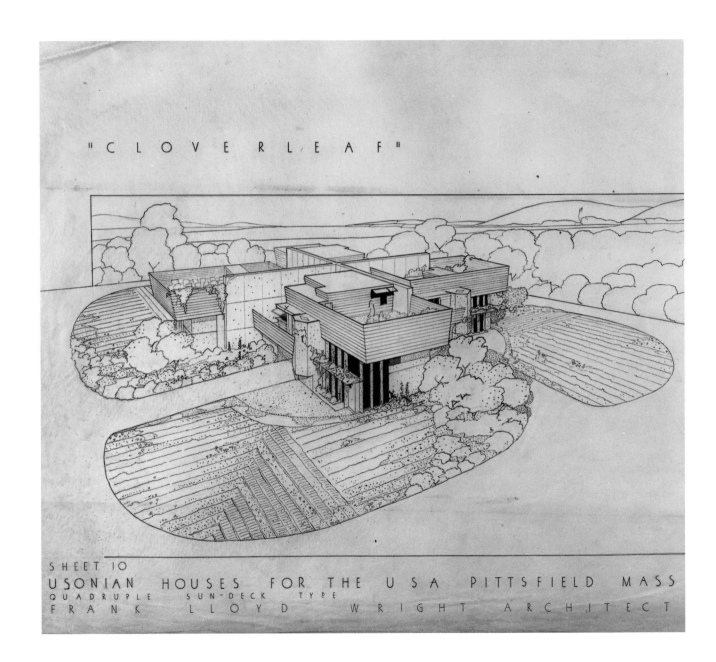

"C L O V E R L E A F"

(Opposite) "Cloverleaf," Frank Lloyd Wright's proposed defense worker housing for the U.S. government, Pittsfield, Massachusetts, 1941

9. WORLD WAR II

We, the undersigned respectfully ask that the Administration of our Government authorize Frank Lloyd Wright to continue the search for Democratic FORM as the basis for a true capitalistic society now known as Broadacre City. We believe that work should immediately be declared a worthy national objective and the necessary ways and means freely granted him to make such plans, models and drawings as will enable our citizens and other peoples to comprehend the basic ideas the plans, models and drawings represent and which, without political bias or influences will be invaluable to our people when peace is being considered.

—Broadacre City Petition to the National Resources Planning Board, February 1943

Throughout his professional life Frank Lloyd Wright complained that he was not given proper recognition in his own land even as he was celebrated with awards from around the world. Given his views on the state of civic architecture in the United States, he could barely contain his contempt for the federal bureaucracy. From the 1920s forward, each encounter with the government was either disappointing or worse, depending on his expectations.

In 1923, while living in California, Wright first encountered Tom Vint, who was chief of the National Park Service planning and design office in Los Angeles. Vint's ideas for Yosemite and other park buildings, a style that came to be known as "government rustic," coincided with Wright's, yet Wright was never hired to work for the National Park Service.

A decade later Wright was seeking out the government, by then filled with people inclined to be receptive to his brand of architecture. In 1931 he had had his secretary, Karl Jensen, send a copy of his Princeton lectures to Franklin Roosevelt. In 1934 he again directed Jensen to write to Roosevelt, this time sending along a copy of *The Disappearing City* and recommending Wright to address a conference on decentralization of industry. These letters have a disingenuous quality, coming from Jensen rather than Wright himself, a sign that Wright either did not take them seriously or, more likely, was protecting himself against the possibility that they would be ignored. He tried once more a year later when he returned from the Washington opening of the Broadacre City exhibit, addressing a letter this time to the first lady as "My dear Madame President."

"Across the lawn from your home in the Corcoran Gallery," he wrote, "is a thoughtful presentation of an idea concerning the situation we face in our country." After explaining the Broadacre City concept, Wright revealed his feelings of rejection:

> Were the models in some gallery in Europe I should not have to write a letter to ask my Queen or my King to see it. To them it would be prophetic and so indispensable. I would be better known to them than I am to you because "no prophet is with honor in his own country"— (you see how modest I am) and so in my own country I ask my madame President (and could I expect my President to see it?) to see the work.

Considered together with his meeting with John Lansill and his radio address in New York, Wright's lobbying efforts on behalf of Broadacre City and the cause for organic architecture were petulant and self-defeating. Wright the artist once again thwarted Wright the promoter and planner. His attitudes were based in part on a misreading of government-sponsored building in Europe. To Wright, Europe was filled with aristocrats who would be hostile to his art. In fact, socialist governments were building housing, but it was practical, spare, and severe, its austerity foreign to Wright's romanticism.

The decentralizing programs launched by the New Deal from 1933 until Roosevelt's campaign for reelection in 1936 did not sit well with powerful interests in big business and on Capitol Hill. Increasingly TVA's social agenda and the prospect of replication for the greenbelt town and rural homestead programs began to fade as the Depression persisted, accompanied by the gathering clouds of war in Europe. Having spent much of the 1910s outside the country, missing the building boom of the 1920s, and then suffering along with the country during the first half of the 1930s, Wright finally found a measure of prosperity and recognition in the late 1930s before the world again plunged into war and Pearl Harbor halted his burgeoning practice.

World War II pitted Japan, Germany, and Italy, the three foreign countries where Wright had lived, against the United States. Bitterly Wright denounced the U.S. government, issuing antiwar tracts in his occasional newsletter, *A Taliesin Square-Paper*. These broadsides, subtitled *A Nonpolitical Voice from Our Democratic Minority*, were in fact the most politicized writing of Wright's career. In January 1941, soon after the Luftwaffe destroyed Coventry, and with St. Michael's cathedral in ruins, Wright advised the stricken British people (whose king had just bestowed on him the Royal Gold Medal for Architecture) that the Blitz provided an opportunity to rebuild.

In a May 29, 1941, exchange with William Evjue, editor of the Madison *Capital Times*, reprinted in the *Square-Paper*, he "deplored the violence of [Evjue's] anti-Hitlerism," condemning Roosevelt's foreign policy

Masthead from *A Taliesin Square-Paper*. Sixteen issues of this broadsheet were published between January 1941 and February 1953.

in a nine-point diatribe against conscription and stating, "I do not believe we are, at present, in more danger within our own nation than from the combined military forces of Germany, France, Italy, Russia and Japan." Railing against Roosevelt, Congress, hasty appropriations for ships and guns, and our alliance with Great Britain and inveighing against the "grand splurge [and] hysterical spending orgy on home-defense," Wright echoed his Uncle Jenkin's and Henry Ford's stand against Woodrow Wilson's war policies. He concluded that the "solution to our world problems in the face of Germany, Russia, France, Italy, and Japan, slave-empire, does lie in the green hills of the Taliesins of our great nation and will be found there if ever found at all."

As political pundit Wright was sharpening his barbs against Roosevelt's defense policies, others were recommending architect Wright to provide plans for defense housing for the government. In a long and revealing account in his *Frank Lloyd Wright Versus America: The 1930s*, Donald Leslie Johnson describes a more reasonable Wright, approached by Clark Foreman, division chief of defense housing, Federal Works Agency (the agency where Frederick Gutheim and Henry Klumb worked). When Foreman called Taliesin long distance, he indicated that Wright's name did not appear on their list of architects. "Why don't you contribute something?" he asked.

"I'd like to, but I've never been asked," was Wright's reply. He later added, "My country has never before called on me. If you are serious and want me to work for you, I will do it and you will be proud of the results." After he had been engaged and a problem arose, Wright was gracious and reassuring: "It is high time I took a hand in governmental building in my own country and co-operation with Dr. Foreman and yourself [Talbot Wegg, the project manager] will be only the beginning...." Selecting a site near Pittsfield, Massachusetts, Wright designed housing using prefabricated precast concrete components. The project, which he called Cloverleaf, was an inventive refinement of his Suntop Homes, built in Ardmore, Pennsylvania, in 1938, consisting of four-unit structures, each with its own entry, two stories, a basement, and a sunroof. The design of Suntop Homes was based on a model constructed for Broadacre City, an alternative to the Usonian house that provided for higher densities and lower costs. Wright's proposal pleased the architects, but House majority leader John McCormack of Massachusetts excoriated Foreman for hiring a Wisconsin architect for a Massachusetts project, and Wright's contract was canceled.

A published account of Wright's second encounter with Washington at war is more bizarre and probably fictitious. An eccentric acquaintance of Wright, Carlton Smith, had a longstanding friendship with Sara Delano Roosevelt, the president's mother, and became an adviser to Roosevelt on matters pertaining to music. Brendan Gill, reading Smith's unpublished memoirs, wrote that Smith recommended Wright to Roosevelt for the design of worker housing at the atomic energy plant at Oak Ridge, Tennessee. According to Gill's account, Wright and Smith went to Washington for a visit to Roosevelt in the Oval Room. As he walked across the threshold, Wright said, "You know, Carlton, I've always told you I would rather be Wright than President," and then addressed the president as "Frank," urging him "to get out of that chair and look around at what they're doing to your city here, miles and miles of Ionic and Corinthian columns!" Given Smith's reputation at Taliesin ("a notorious name-dropper," according to Bruce Brooks Pfeiffer), the veracity of his anecdote is questionable. If the story is true, it suggests that the contact with Roosevelt was casual rather than substantive. First, they met in the Oval Room, which was located in Roosevelt's family quarters at the White House, the place where he met friends and mixed martinis, rather than the Oval Office, where he conducted business. If he had been serious, he would probably have had an expert present, someone involved in the ultra-top-secret Oak Ridge project, and he probably would have known that Wright was being investigated at the time by the FBI for his antiwar pronouncements.

Manufactured housing at Oak Ridge was critical, requiring a rate of construction that peaked at 40 houses per day for scientists and workers fabricating the experiments that would lead to the atomic bomb and nuclear power. The architects selected for the project included John Merrill of Skidmore, Owings and Merrill, who had been engaged in other sensitive government projects, and government planner Tracy Auger, formerly with Albert Kahn's Detroit office and recently a planner at Norris Village, which was only 16 miles away.

Wright's efforts to promote Broadacre City continued without pause. In the summer of 1936 he sent Gene Masselink on a trip along the east coast. Among others Masselink sought out Lewis Mumford (to engage his support for a Broadacre City demonstration at the 1939 World's Fair), Albert Einstein in Princeton, John Nicholas Brown in Providence, and Mrs. Avery Coonley, a former Wright client. Wright also maintained a constant correspondence with developers, builders, bankers, and building supply manufacturers, many of whom pledged support when prosperity returned. After the war began, Wright stepped up his efforts to gain Roosevelt's attention, making a presentation before Frederic Delano and the National Resources Planning Board in February 1943, followed by a petition to Delano. The Broadacre City petition, a typically Wrightian exercise in futility, was signed by more than 60 prominent friends and clients. A few who were asked to sign, such as Albert Einstein, declined. Wright had made substantial efforts to enlist every famous person he knew. Sending the Broadacre City prospectus to Vice President Henry Wallace, Wright indicated, "This is to you personally, not as a government official." Wallace replied that he "liked the [Broadacre City idea] immensely," but he treated it as an intellectual exercise rather than a practical project: "I am passing it on to the Spanish poet, [Juan Ramón] Jiménez, who thinks along somewhat the same lines."

To Hollywood screenwriter Marc Connelly, Wright acknowledged a message from his son Lloyd that Connelly had promised to sign the petition, asking him to enlist "a few [Hollywood] directors René Clair, Preston Sturges (the bastard never answers me), John Ford, Richard Day—just a few feathers, because the creative citizenry is a blackout just now." Wright also mentioned Orson Welles, whom he had recently met on the set of *The Magnificent Ambersons* where Welles was directing Wright's granddaughter, Anne Baxter. Welles did not sign the petition. During the same week Wright also wrote to Robert Moses, whose wife was Wright's cousin, and to Archibald MacLeish, the Librarian of Congress and a genuine friend of Wright's. When he heard, a few weeks after the petition was sent, that the National Resources Planning Board had been abolished, Wright wrote to Delano, hoping for some kind of endorsement. "I do not know what the Board could do for me except to give me its blessing and good speed."

One can only guess at Wright's motives at this point. A likely explanation relates to the republication of his *Autobiography*, the third of a suite of books published by Duell, Sloan and Pearce in New York. The first, Frederick Gutheim's *Frank Lloyd Wright on Architecture*, had been published in 1941. The second volume, Wright's revised *Autobiography*, was to appear in fall 1941, followed by Henry-Russell Hitchcock's *In the*

Nature of Materials, in the winter of 1941–42. In fact, Hitchcock's book came out later in 1942, and Wright was still working on his book in late February 1943. Obviously, publicity regarding Broadacre City not only could help the sales of the book, but could help convince the publishers to include "Book Six: Broadacre City," which was, in fact, not included. Instead, the Broadacre City chapter was issued as an offprint by Taliesin a few months later. During 1945 the University of Chicago Press published Wright's revision of *The Disappearing City* with a new, patriotic title, *When Democracy Builds.* It was revised and republished with new material later in 1945 and reprinted in 1947 and 1951. A 1945 British edition was also published. In 1957 Wright substantially rewrote the Broadacre City proposal, adding new plans and renderings, for republication as *The Living City* by Horizon Press in 1958, with a Japanese edition published in Toyko in 1968. Finally, in 1969, Horizon Press published a facsimile edition, an annotated *Disappearing City,* indicating revisions by Wright's hand, and with a complete revised text and a new title: *The Industrial Revolution Runs Away.* Only 1,250 hand-numbered copies were published.

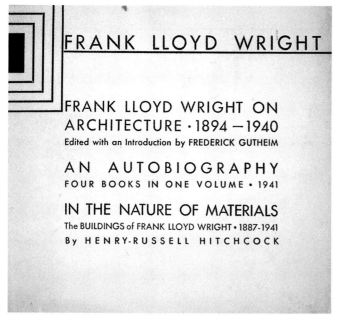

Sales brochure from Duell, Sloan and Pearce promoting three books, issued upon publication of the first, Frederick Gutheim's *Frank Lloyd Wright on Architecture*

As the war ended, many of Wright's apprentices, who had been either drafted into service or jailed for their refusal, returned to Taliesin. Rudi Mock, returning from service with the OSS in London, moved to Knoxville with his wife Betty, assuming the position with TVA that had been vacated by Roland Wank. Henry Klumb, who had gone to Puerto Rico in 1941 with Rexford Tugwell when Tugwell went to serve as territorial governor, returned to Washington to assist the Greenbelt, Maryland, cooperative in its efforts to buy out the government's interest. Later he returned to Puerto Rico and became the island's leading architect.

The defeat of Axis forces brought the GIs home, creating an instant, pressing need for low-cost family housing across the United States. Experiments during the war, particularly in the Tennessee Valley, pointed the way to a new type of manufactured housing and to industrial methods of mass construction. *Architectural Forum* led the way in its efforts to bridge the gap between the travel trailer industry and manufacturers of prefabricated houses. According to Allen Wallis, "Although there were parallel developments...from the 1930s through the war years, minimal exchanges took place between the two. One exception was the development of a transportable house for the Tennessee Valley Authority."

One quarter of all American housing constructed during World War II, over 200,000 units, was factory built. TVA's Fontana Dam Village was the first community of prefabricated dwellings in the country. The houses were proposed in 1937 by TVA architect Louis Grangent and further developed by Carroll A. Towne. They were built in 1940 at the same time the Rosenbaum house was going up, just across the river in a Sheffield, Alabama, factory, then trucked in two sections to the site at a cost of about $2,000 a copy. These houses were also later shipped to England after the London Blitz and were used at Oak Ridge. They were

25'8"-by-13'6" one-bedroom houses with a flat, deep-eaved roof and picture window, a caricature of the Usonian house that cost less than half as much, a minimal, temporary solution to a pressing need.

The two-part TVA house of 1940 showed the influence of much of Wright's work: his Prairie Style houses and his American System Readi-Cut structures; the House on the Mesa concept drawings and the Willey house; the Hoult and Lusk projects; the Jacobs and Rosenbaum houses and the more minimal Goetsche-Winckler house; the Suntops in Ardmore and their near-miss government successors in Pittsfield. These design ideas were blended with European modernism and with manufacturing techniques pioneered by Henry Ford and concepts developed for the travel trailer in the late 1910s. Because they were transported by truck from a factory site, they had to be light, small, and easy to construct. Like the Usonians, the TVA trailer houses were made of plywood. Unlike the Usonians, they were tiny, more like a ship's cabin and a Pullman compartment than a house. They contained a small living room with a bay window an even smaller bedroom, bathroom with shower, and a kitchen with doorways into the other three rooms.

In 1940 small prefabricated houses were designed and built at Muscle Shoals for workers at the dam sites, and, later, for defense workers.

Eventually this completely new type of housing would evolve into the mobile home, an industry born in the housing shortage after World War II, maturing as the most ubiquitous low-cost house in America by 1960, its manufacturing scattered across the Midwest, including several factories in north Alabama. When the mobile house was actually put into production, first by the U.S. government and later in private industry, architects, clients, and critics were appalled by their ugliness, the low quality of their materials, their ungainly design, and the parks in which they were sited. But unlike public housing projects or greenbelt superblocks,

Prefabricated houses on site near Fontana dam, transported from Muscle Shoals, August 1943

the mobile home was popular because it allowed for individuality. These 10-foot-wide, then "double-wide" single-family dwellings were individually owned and often sited on owner-occupied land; models were available in colors with differing materials, decors, and layouts; the houses were often "built out" with the addition of a mudroom, cabana, or patio, or an additional bedroom or workshop added at a later time. Finally, mobile houses were unlike site-built houses in that they were purchased as all-inclusive units—furniture and appliances included with a single payment to the bank or finance company—and they could be moved when their owner relocated or decided to sell, a merger of automobility with convenience, the essence of Broadacre City.

Obviously Wright did not foresee or appreciate the housing revolution in this form. In fact, he took his ideas for low-cost, on-site prefabrication in another direction with panelized manufactured houses, a business venture with Marshall Erdman, an architect-builder in Madison, Wisconsin. Although they attempted economies of scale, the effort was a disaster, resulting in the construction of only two houses. According to Erdman, Wright was untutored in administration, finance, organization, and management and was creating a system "where the details were not geared to production. He simply did not know how to do prefabrication."

By the 1950s Wright had admitted that his houses were for the "upper middle third of the democratic strata of our country," but continued to look for ways to cut basic costs, insisting that by replacing the plywood sandwich walls of the Usonian house with an on-site fabricated block, and with a factory-made package of plumbing, heating, and wiring "easily installed by making several simple connections," costs would be significantly reduced. These Usonian Automatics were first constructed for clients living near Taliesin West (the Adelman and Pieper residences, 1951–52), with a construction method derived from Wright's Biltmore

Hotel cottages, the Millard house, and his other California concrete-block houses of the 1920s. In *The Natural House* (1954) Wright presented the Usonian Automatic as a natural extension of his prototype Usonians—depicting the Willey, Jacobs, Sturges, and Goetsch-Winkler houses, Suntop Homes, the Cloverleaf project, and the Rosenbaum house in succession—before moving on to his stock-in-trade postwar Usonians that combined textile-block features with wood and stone, as in the Miller (1946) and Brauner (1948) houses. Wright presented his final word on Usonians with a do-it-yourself explanation of forming steel-rod-reinforced textile blocks on site. Despite his claim, virtually none of the Automatics were low cost. Beginning in the 1940s Wright received several commissions for Usonian ensembles, including his four Parkwyn Village houses (1947) in Kalamazoo; those in Okemos and Galesburg, Michigan; and, notably, a collaboration with the young engineer David Henken in Pleasantville, New York, for a site plan they called Usonia Homes. Henken had been drawn to Wright's ideas for Broadacre City and the Usonian house when he saw the 1940 Museum of Modern Art exhibition and had become a Taliesin apprentice in 1942. He incorporated a cooperative plan with the

Usonian Automatic (Turkel residence), Detroit, Michigan, under construction, 1954

state of New York in 1944 for which he located a 97-acre site in Westchester County by 1947. As construction began—with some houses designed by Wright, some by Henken, some by other architects—a complex financing scheme was developed. Complete common ownership of land and houses for 50 families proved impractical, but a group mortgage with 99-year leases back to the owners was worked out with an enlightened banker. However limited, Usonia Homes was the only true test of Broadacre City principles in the real world. It incorporated the concept of design review with cooperative land ownership and a democratic community government in a setting removed from the city. By 1985 David Henken would write that "modifications and outright abrogation have become the norm. Despite the resultant community and individual trauma possibly engendered by these actions, a community of remarkable stability has grown to maturity."

The culmination of the mature Usonians and all of Wright's Michigan experiments can be found in his house for Mary and William Palmer in Ann Arbor, perhaps the highest expression of his Usonian art. The

Site plan for Usonia Homes in Pleasantville, New York, 1947

Palmer house was not, however, a solution to the small house problem. By 1950, having struggled through the 1930s and 1940s with schemes for limiting costs while maintaining quality, designing houses for families with incomes falling into the solid middle of the middle third (a population segment many times larger than those with upper-middle incomes), Wright finally recognized his niche and accepted only projects that were adequately funded. On April 17, 1950, Mary Palmer wrote to Wright that she and her husband had purchased an acre of land outside Ann Arbor, had visited many Wright-designed homes in Michigan, and had "been stimulated" by reading his books. She expressed the hope "that we will not have to compromise in selecting a lesser architect...to design the home we wish to build next year." The deciding moment for the Palmers was their visit to the Affleck house in Bloomfield Hills on the far side of Detroit, an exemplary Usonian built by Gregor and Elizabeth Affleck in 1940. "Their advice to us was simple: give Mr. Wright a budget of only half of what you plan to spend." With an initial announced budget of $30,000 and a final cost near $50,000, the Palmer house was not intended to be a kit of parts, but instead, a site-specific, elegantly detailed, warm, and beautiful house for gracious living for a university economics professor, his musician wife, and their two children.

10. TODAY AND TOMORROW

Frank Lloyd Wright's life was a jumble of contradictions. He was a radical who often sounded like an arch-conservative; he loved order and rational, efficient planning, yet conducted parts of his life in complete disarray; he mixed a tough, disciplined style of working and living with a self-indulgent love of luxury, often sending what seemed to be a mixed message to his students, clients, and creditors. Wright's architecture was rooted in the American Midwest but derived a universal appeal from its incorporation of Mayan, Javanese, Byzantine, and Japanese as well as native American forms. His work belongs to the highest order of original creation, yet he was able and willing to integrate the ideas of others.

Another seeming contradiction in Wright's career is that between the romantic, steeped in 19th-century American individualism, and the modern man, always looking to the next wave of progress. In fact, Wright integrated his past so completely into his life's work that it is easy not to see it. He was born in Richland Center, Wisconsin, in 1867 and was buried 92 years later at Taliesin, only a few minutes away, where he lived most of his life on the land his mother's ancestors had settled generations before. Until his body was moved to Taliesin West after Olgivanna's death in 1985, Wright was interred in the cemetery next to the Jones family chapel, designed by J. Lyman Silsbee, his first employer and a close friend of his Uncle Jenkin Lloyd-Jones. He attended the University of Wisconsin, in his home town of Madison, where two members of his family served as trustees. When he moved to Chicago, he remained close to his uncle, married the daughter of a family friend, and brought his mother to Oak Park to live with them. Even after his first marriage broke up, Wright remained faithful to his home place, returning to Spring Green to build a new home for his mistress and his mother.

Wright's genius was to sense the winds of change at first hint and to give form to ideas through a conveyance that was both very simple and highly complex. Like Henry Ford, he belonged to an era that took leadership seriously, an idealistic, evangelistic, moralistic generation. Their contemporaries were reformers Emma Goldman, W. E. B. DuBois, Margaret Sanger, and Jane Addams; revivalist Billy Sunday; publisher William Randolph Hearst; writers and muckrakers Theodore Dreiser, H. L. Mencken, and Upton Sinclair; inventors Wilbur and Orville Wright; dancer Isadora Duncan; statesmen Gandhi, Churchill, Lenin, and Roosevelt; Albert Schweitzer; Albert Einstein; Pablo Picasso. According to historians William Strauss and Neil

Howe, the members of this generation were under the strong influence of their mothers: "the indulged children of the Gilded Age…[raised in a] controlled but pleasantly free atmosphere." As Richard Hofstadter wrote of Henry Ford, the political ideas many of them carried forward were the most innocent and least radical planks from the old platforms of agrarian revolt.

As an architect, Wright was an original. As a planner, working on a landscape that included politicians and social scientists, he was an integrator of ideas, less certain of his ground, more liable to stumble, much like other planners who must face everyday realities. As he conceived new patterns of development he ignored the art of the possible. Planning by its nature is inextricably tied to local political and economic realities, where the conventional wisdom of powerful forces—what he saw as "specious authority"—reigns over individuality.

The problem of transforming Wright's vision into reality was not in any misunderstanding of the future of automobility or of communications networks, but in his underestimation of the effects of the Depression and of the immutability of Americans' belief in their ancestral myths and myth-making institutions. For those who are struggling, decent shelter supersedes other concerns: the ugliness of public housing and mobile homes, the monotony of the housing in the greenbelt towns and postwar Levittowns was unimportant when measured against simple demand for availability and affordability. For the more affluent—which was always Wright's clientele—Frederick Olmsted's vision, which followed Andrew Jackson Downing's vision, which followed Thomas Jefferson's vision, back into the English countryside, has remained incredibly steadfast over the course of American history.

Wright failed as a planner but succeeded as a visionary, imagining a place where, to use a Bertrand Russell phrase, "creative rather than possessive impulses [were] uppermost." At Broadacre City, greed was replaced by a communitarian spirit under the moral leadership of the architect-poet, the community transformed into Hugo's cathedral. Ultimately Wright saw organic architecture as lifting the individual out of the tyranny of conformity to accepted tastes, providing a new "embodiment of human freedom." By the late 1950s, when he refined the Broadacre plan in *The Living City*, he returned to architecture as the motive force of planning, replacing most of the diatribes against congestion and urban form with a more positive exposition for Broadacre City.

In an era that predated the concept of civil rights as we know it, Broadacre City stood for equality. Wright was highly opinionated on matters relating to the arts, but as an artist he looked beyond race, religion, politics, gender, or nationality to find the qualities that defined an individual. Wright was troubled by competition among religions and sought to find a common bond between East and West, the emotional, earth-loving eastern faiths and the more intellectual Judeo-Christian tradition. The Broadacre City of Frank Lloyd Wright was unquestionably based on American values and culture, a blend of ethnicity with the vernacular at its grass roots, a combination reflecting the diversity of his own household.

This vision of an integrated, cooperative, spiritual community of like-minded interests, a blending into a single American culture, is one of the least understood aspects of the Broadacre plan. At Broadacre City, Usonians gathered in fellowship at parks and galleries, at schools and universities, zoos, arboretums, libraries, theaters, cinemas, planetariums, community centers, golf courses, lakes, picnic areas, and in nonsectarian churches, located at each concentration at the county seat. As at Taliesin, voluntary, cheerful service to the community was its strength. Given Wright's interests, participation in the arts played a larger role in Broadacre City than was generally the case in cities.

While the town plan on the middle landscape of Broadacre City encouraged a call for community, the architecture that housed the family unit itself was a paraphrase of the whole. The interplay between individual and community spheres across a landscape found a metaphor within the universe of the small Wright house. The zones within a house reflected the zones in the community; hallways, streets; living rooms, gathering places; gardens, parks.

If nothing else is clear about Frank Lloyd Wright's philosophy, certainly his love of nature and his nurturing concern for its protection are evident from his earliest enunciation of his ideas. In Broadacre City he isolated large-scale manufacturing enterprises, their products to be distributed underground when possible. (Wright, having praised Henry Ford and his architect Albert Kahn on many occasions, believed that the factory "is already so well organized, built, and managed that it needs less redesigning than any enterprising unit we have.") In the early 1950s, before its hazards were generally known, he also endorsed peaceful uses of nuclear power as a nonpolluting, renewable source of energy.

For Wright, "architecture and acreage together [were] landscape.... We seek beauty of landscape not so much to build upon—as to build with." The integration of site and structure was fundamental to organic principles. As the indoor-outdoor qualities of Usonian houses glorified nature, their construction method sought the least invasion of the soil. At the Rosenbaum construction site, excavation was kept to a minimum.

Without a basement and without a deep frost line, footings and slab were laid shallow, a few steps added here and there as the site sloped gently south. Once a field for corn or cotton, the Rosenbaums' lot had only a few trees at the edges, away from the structure's footprint.

Like Franklin Roosevelt, Wright was deeply influenced by landscape traditions that developed in the Hudson Valley and New England in the second half of the 19th century, a romantic ideal conceived by Henry David Thoreau and John Burroughs, painted by Frederic Church and Thomas Cole, and given physical form by Andrew Jackson Downing and Frederick Olmsted. At Hyde Park and Spring Green, both saw themselves as farmers in the tradition of Thomas Jefferson, scientific, independent, and public spirited; and both were influenced early in their careers by Progressive politicians—Wright by La Follette, Roosevelt by Pinchot—who believed in the government's careful stewardship of the nation's natural resources.

If Wright had followed Nancy Willey's suggestion that he should read H. G. Wells's futuristic work in 1934 when he was designing Broadacre City, he would have discovered predictions of a widely scattered metropolis, with an "entertaining agglomeration" of shops and concourses, and pedestrian pathways along thoroughfares. (In fact the wayside markets in Broadacre City anticipated, as planning historian Robert Fishman suggests, modern-day shopping malls.) By 1958, when *The Living City* was published, ebullient prosperity had completely replaced 1930s desperation. Americans had bailed out of rural poverty after the war. Of the 25.8 million who lived on farms in 1947, fewer than 10 million remained by 1970. At the same time, urban factory workers moved with their jobs and the growth of their families out to the suburbs, leaving the shell of their inner-city life for the unemployed and underclass of society. Ever-more-affluent bedroom communities sprouted office towers and shopping malls hugged the big cities along eight-lane thoroughfares, as the automobile stretched the idea of suburbia into a whole new pattern of unplanned development.

Places like Tysons Corner, Virginia, near Washington, D.C.; Buckhead, near Atlanta; and Detroit's Northland Mall area grew up in fields outside large cities, a devil of mixed use called technoburbs, slurbs, and edge cities. The difference between these developments and the suburbs has been the attempt by land developers to bring jobs and shopping to where people live, the opposite of suburbia of old, where residents boarded streetcars and trains or drove their automobiles downtown to work or shop. Like greenbelt towns and the mass housing projects in the 1930s, these unpretty places, often at the intersection of two interstate highways, make it possible to travel laterally from work to home to shopping, without venturing either into the city or out to the countryside. While their transportation nodes are similar to those of Broadacre City, the whole concept is city-dependent and built on land speculation, large enterprises, and impersonal national franchising, the antithesis of Broadacre City. An accompanying technology—computers, cable television, cellular telephones, automated tellers—has fostered centripetal growth of these new cities encircling old cities. These neo-frontiers, in fact, are already old frontiers based on capital-intensive technology and dependent on large concentrations of high-density development. Growth in these places resulted from a one-time leap in population, as postwar baby-boomers entered house-buying maturity.

The new technologies of telecommunication have created a distributive society that is no longer tied to the city, and these geo-independent patterns of growth continue to promote decentralization in an era with a smaller pool of first-time home buyers and an increasingly larger percentage of couples whose children have left home and who are moving toward a scaled-down style of living and retirement. While unlinking many kinds of work from the city, the new technologies are also changing the nature of work, eliminating the tedium of busy-work tasks and drudgery from many kinds of jobs, permitting more interaction between people, more time to think. They encourage individual autonomy, a development that Wright would have applauded. They also support environmental sensitivity and the conservation of natural resources, encouraging energy-efficient commuting, recyclable packaging, and nonpolluting industry.

Although the Usonian house was generic, the qualities of each house and site reflect the locale. The Rosenbaum house did indeed provide a local architecture of local materials. The brick was baked in kilns down the road in Decatur from north Alabama red clay. Cypress was also local, growing in the swampy marshes along Cypress Creek not far from the house, although the actual lumber and plywood for the house may have come from a Florida mill. But the form and materials of the Rosenbaum house were essentially the same as those of the Hoult, Lusk, and Jacobs houses, prototypes rooted in Kansas, South Dakota, and Wisconsin. This juxtaposition of the specific with the universal is a blend of regional with national qualities that does not diminish either. With today's modern communications and mobility, these qualities are complementary. The danger now is the opposite of the danger of a generation ago. A local or regional culture that once struggled to be more cosmopolitan now risks losing its character and its locally based economy in the bland sameness of franchise businesses, forgetting its special qualities in pursuit of what is perceived as a better American way.

In 1940 Frank Lloyd Wright would have found it hard to believe that 40 million people would be working from their homes at least part of the time, as evidenced by tax returns declaring a home office deduction in 1990. When Wright placed a sanctum or study off the living room in his first Usonian houses, he envisioned professors grading papers, journalists writing stories, businessmen toting figures in a room sufficiently removed yet close enough for brief interruption. As women have assumed an equal role in the nation's work life, the integration of activities at home perhaps now exceeds the expectations of Broadacre City. This is particularly true of Wright's constituency for the Usonian house: *Builder* magazine reported in 1990 that more than half of home workers have college degrees and one in five postgraduate degrees, and that they earn a household income that is more than $10,000 greater than the national average.

Since Wright's time Americans have become more aware of both the built and the natural environments. The environmental and preservation movements in the United States have begun to merge, together contributing to a new sensibility regarding our landscape and creating common ground for responsible public policies. Americans have also become more conscious of design. Corporate and government commitment to improving design in the 1950s and 1960s has encouraged a better appreciation of design as organic: as Nancy Hanks, the first chairman of the National Endowment for the Arts, put it, "not an add-on...[but] part of the essence of the thing."

Frank Lloyd Wright's vision for America, while impossible to achieve in the desperate 1930s, has helped to give shape to America for the 21st century. The outlines of Usonia have been drawn. In places like Muscle Shoals, in Alabama, or a remote stretch of Arizona desert, the promise of a better life beckons as an idea at least as old as Broadacre City begins to find its ground. In its physical form—its layout and architecture—

this Usonia appears somewhat different from Wright's, but its ideas are the same: the sensible use of technology to diminish the toil of work; a respect for the environment and for the beauty of its vistas; the conservation of natural resources; the harmonizing of work and pleasure, social, family, and working relationships into one; the coalescing of nationalities in America with cooperation in community activity and participation in the arts; a peaceful coexistence and free exchange across cultures and national boundaries; a respect for individuality and a love of craftsmanship; a commitment to education and an appreciation for things made beautiful; and a deep feeling for the contributions of our ancestors and the value of our history in shaping the future.

■

Usonian houses have begun to reach their prime: The first Jacobs residence, the Rosenbaum house, and the 1939 residences have passed the half-century mark, while many of the others will reach 50 before the end of the 20th century. These houses convincingly tell the story of our nation's prosperity, a standard set to house families with incomes in the upper half of America's middle third, the group that built the ranch-style house in suburban communities across the country. In recent years Taliesin Associates Architects has supervised the construction of a number of Usonian houses that had been designed during Wright's lifetime but had not been built by the original clients. As livable, gracious, and beautiful houses, they remain as suitable for suburban and exurban family life today as they were 50 years ago.

The principal obstacles to constructing a Usonian house today relate to cost and to local building codes. Usonian houses were made of natural materials with a considerable degree of craftsmanship, both which were relatively available and inexpensive during the last years before World War II. After the war, new materials and labor-saving approaches began to take over, as housing developments incorporated fast-track and assembly line techniques to meet the extraordinary demand for new single-family houses on the fringes of large and middle-size cities. As Usonians were built into the 1950s, their locations tended to be in rural areas, on the outskirts of small cities or in smaller towns. Over time, however, these houses have been influential in the evolution of the suburban house in America in a variety of ways. Certainly the open, flowing spaces of a Usonian house can be found in almost any contemporary suburban house, along with cathedral ceilings, the extensive use of wood and natural finishes, the return of the fireplace, outdoor access from different rooms, built-in furniture and cabinetry to create a sense of space, the integration of design elements, and, outside, carports, patios, and natural landscaping.

The functional aspects of the Usonian house have had an even greater influence than its aesthetics. Frank Lloyd Wright pioneered an approach for zoning, separating various functions—individual and group, day and night, light and dark—and collecting mechanical and structural elements into modules that combined rational construction methods with the advantages of expandability. As a kit of parts, Usonians were easily expanded, and many were adapted by Wright for his original clients. This feature also became a characteristic of American suburban houses as growing families and growing incomes demanded additions of family rooms, bedrooms, and bathrooms.

Moreover, the Usonian prototype itself was adjusted in one way that anticipated the contemporary suburban house. Because the majority of Wright's clients included married women who did not work outside the home and had either no domestic help or only part-time assistance, the kitchen and laundry were at first organized simply. From a range of comments from Wright's Usonian clients, it was generally agreed that the early kitchen units were too small. By the time the Rosenbaums built their addition, the kitchen had been expanded to include more room for storage and work space for more than one person.

Site planning was also deeply influenced by the Usonians. Wright's radical departure from the norm in turning the back of the house to the street at first seemed antisocial in many neighborhoods where Usonian houses were built. Over time, other architects and builders adopted the Wright style of site planning, placing houses close to the front of the lot and providing a relatively closed front facade with a wide open back, where most of the property could be used for gardening, children's play, and family privacy. Wright's use of the natural contours of a site—a few steps here and there to help to delineate zones and provide variation—has been adapted by contemporary builders, particularly when faced with a difficult site condition.

The celebration of the architectural works of Frank Lloyd Wright and their preservation as national landmarks suggests a vindication of Wright's design for America. As prototypes for the mid-century American "dream house," Usonian houses have become national treasures, beautifully crafted examples that inspired thousands of builders and hundreds of thousands of homeowners as an accessible, advanced, purely American form of domestic architecture, offering a new definition of luxury and convenience for rising standards of living in the postwar era.

In 1978 the Rosenbaum house was placed in the National Register of Historic Places. In 1989, celebrating its 50th anniversary, an open house was held for the Florence community, sponsored by Heritage Preservation and the Florence Historical Board, two local preservation groups, and drawing over 1,000 people to see the house that day. In 1991 Mildred Rosenbaum was honored by the Frank Lloyd Wright Building Conservancy with one of its first Wright Spirit Awards. It was given in recognition of her devotion to the principles of organic architecture, her expertise in the works of Frank Lloyd Wright, and for her longevity, having maintained her Wright house longer than any other client. Mildred Rosenbaum continues to live and work in her Frank Lloyd Wright house, conducting daily tours by appointment for visitors from all over the country. In 1992 the Frank Lloyd Wright Rosenbaum House Foundation was organized by members of the Florence community to assist preservation of the house and to promote education relating to the work of Frank Lloyd Wright.

In the Muscle Shoals area of Alabama, the Usonian legacy is half realized. Along the Tennessee River, from Court Street, the main thoroughfare east to Wilson Dam, the promenade of Water Street is littered with abandoned sheds, marginal industrial sites, and substandard housing. Virtually no one lives or walks along the river bluff, which is lost in a tangle of overgrowth along the old railroad right of way. In downtown Florence, the old storefronts and graceful neighborhoods remain as reminders of the past, but the promises of Henry Ford and TVA have faded as industry peaked in the 1960s, then slowly declined.

Stately antebellum mansions and clean TVA lakes, barbecue and catfish, sweet soul music and thick southern accents still define Muscle Shoals. In this area, with its natural beauty and inexpensive land, its temperate climate, and its resources, the promise of 75 Mile City-cum-Broadacre City is alive and well. The vision of Andrew Jackson, the stubbornness of Theodore Roosevelt, the dreams of Henry Ford and Arthur Morgan, the ideas of Frank Lloyd Wright, all frame the possibilities for places like Muscle Shoals: small businesses linked to the rest of the world by telecommunications and interstate highways, three hours by car or an hour by air from the big city; heritage tourism; entertainment that reminds us of our past and its stake in our future; water recreation—fishing and boating on TVA lakes; affordable housing for retirees; community theater; and home-grown music. Away from the city and suburbs, other communities that offer the qualities of Broadacre City will begin to grow as high prices, congestion, and dangerous streets together with the potential of communications and transportation technologies begin to permit workers a much wider choice in places to work, live, and raise their families.

The challenge for Usonia now is the development of leadership in those communities to protect what is valuable, to plan in a manner that protects the environment and the treasures from the past. The dawning of this effort has begun with efforts of the National Park Service and with local initiatives—such as TVA's River Heritage Program—which create frameworks for planners and citizens to develop heritage areas that preserve natural, recreational, and cultural resources, crossing jurisdictional boundaries and forging new community relationships that are more cooperative than competitive. As an organizing principle, regionalism and heritage areas provide the next best hope for the understanding of the legacy of Broadacre City and of Frank Lloyd Wright's design for America.

EPILOGUE

December 12, 1991, Washington, D.C. At the Smithsonian Museum of American History five gray eminences of Usonia gathered at the center of the cavernous marble foyer for a photo opportunity and reception after their panel discussion on the Usonian houses of Frank Lloyd Wright: Edgar Tafel, a 1932 charter member of the Taliesin Fellowship; Professor John Sergeant, a Cambridge don and architect, author of the authoritative *Frank Lloyd Wright's Usonian Houses*; architectural historian and Wright expert Richard Guy Wilson from the University of Virginia; Loren Pope of Washington, who built the Usonian house now owned by the National Trust for Historic Preservation as the Pope-Leighey House; and Tom Casey, dean of the Frank Lloyd Wright School of Architecture and a member of the Taliesin community since 1950.

At the other end of the foyer, a majestic figure of George Washington, sculpted in 1840 by Horatio Greenough, officiated over the assembly. Greenough's Washington is seated on a throne, clad in a toga, his left hand offering a sword, his right hand raised, a finger pointed to the heavens. Ironically, it was Greenough the essayist who was the first critic of American architecture to relate form with function, the foundation of modernism, Louis Sullivan's "form follows function," and then Frank Lloyd Wright's "form and function are one." In his treatise "Form and Function," Greenough predicted, "These United States are destined to form a new style of architecture," and presented an enduring idea:

> The law of adaptation is the fundamental law of nature in all structure....The edifices in whose construction the principles of architecture are developed may be classed as organic, formed to meet the wants of their occupants, or monumental, addressed to the sympathies, the faith, or the taste of a people.

George Washington by Horatio Greenough, 1840

At one end of the Smithsonian hall, the proponents of organic architecture were posed in a tableau; at the other end, the monumental George Washington was seated in repose, looking ridiculous, yet also as solid as a post office, an embodiment of traditional American partialities, providing another version of

America's sensibility. The Smithsonian's giant pendulum swung back and forth between the two, marking alternating inspirational visions of how we live and should live. For Daniel Burnham and Franklin Roosevelt, Greenough's prediction of a new American architecture translated lofty ideals that were rooted in England and Europe into civic design writ large and firm—boastful, ageless, and commanding. For Frank Lloyd Wright, the forms and colors of nature were the fabric for Usonia, a modern vision that balanced landscape with the machine and a mobile citizenry, its power subtle but penetrating.

The monuments of these alternative Americas remain, but their meaning is obscured. Architects move between them, to and fro, like the Smithsonian pendulum, seeking somehow to synthesize the two, a summary without a conclusion. Planners also struggle to find the golden mean between exciting city streets and the pastoral peace of the countryside, fighting uncontrolled sprawl at the edge that joins the worst of both into interminable traffic against an ungainly foreground. But among the jumble new forms will emerge, perhaps giving us a vision for a renewed American civilization.

NOTES

Sources for direct quotations are cited by page number.

Introduction
23 "The curious circumstances": Elizabeth Walter, "Frank Lloyd Wright in Alabama," *Apelles* 2 (1982): 30–35.

1 Unity
25 "The science of printing": Frank Lloyd Wright, *The Future of Architecture* (New York: Horizon Press, 1953), 67. 26 "Honorable people": Maginel Wright Barney, *The Valley of the God-Almighty Joneses* (Spring Green, Wis.: Unity Chapel Publications, 1965), 18–19; "Well-to-do farmers": quoted in Richard Hofstadter, *The Age of Reform* (New York: Random House, 1955), 132. 28 "Book fodder": Frank Lloyd Wright, "Books That Have Meant Most to Me," *Scholastic*, September 24, 1932, 11; "The best amateur essay": ibid.; "Architecture was the principal...form": Victor Hugo, *The Hunchback of Notre Dame* (New York: Penguin Books, 1965), 186. 30 "Pander[s] to silly women: quoted in Robert C. Twombly, *Frank Lloyd*

Wright: An Interpretive Biography (New York: Harper and Row, 1973), 45. 31 "Prospect and refuge": Grant Hildebrand, *The Wright Space* (Seattle: University of Washington Press, 1991), 16; "Every architectural episode": quoted in Herbert Muschamp, *Man About Town: Frank Lloyd Wright in New York City* (Cambridge, Mass.: MIT Press, 1983), 75; "The damage wrought": Louis H. Sullivan, *The Autobiography of an Idea* (New York: Dover Publications, 1956), 325. 31–33 "Just half a century earlier": Henry Steele Commager, *The American Mind* (New Haven: Yale University Press, 1950), 396. 33 "The first expression of American thought," etc.: Henry Adams, *The Education of Henry Adams* (Boston: Houghton Mifflin Company, 1961), 340. 34–35 "Individualism": quoted in Commager, *The American Mind*, 296. 38 "The center of Bitter Root": Donald Leslie Johnson, *Frank Lloyd Wright versus America: The 1930s* (Cambridge, Mass.: MIT Press, 1990), 147; "I was losing grip," etc.: Frank Lloyd Wright, *An Autobiography* (New York: Duell, Sloan and Pearce, 1943), 162–163. 39 "The 'United States'": Frank Lloyd Wright, *A Testament* (New

York: Horizon Press, 1957), 160. 41 "Persecuted...pursued": Wright, *Autobiography*, 166; "Fictitious semblances": in Frederick Gutheim, ed., *Frank Lloyd Wright on Architecture* (New York: Grosset and Dunlap, 1951), 48; "Alone in my field": ibid., 46–47; "His first proclamation": Twombly, *Frank Lloyd Wright*, 127. 42–43 "At a richness and complexity": Henry-Russell Hitchcock, *In the Nature of Materials* (New York: Duell, Sloan and Pearce, 1942), caption to plate 191.

2 Muscle Shoals
45 "Compensation for all work": Herman V. von Holst and Frank Lloyd Wright, contract, September 22, 1909, Frank Lloyd Wright Home and Studio Archives. 46 "He remembers": Grant Manson, *Frank Lloyd Wright to 1910* (New York: Van Nostrand Reinhold, 1958), 213; "What on earth": quoted in *Detroit News-Tribune*, July 11, 1913, p. 5. 48 "Edsel might have discussed": E. G. Liebold, oral history, 1951, 27, Henry Ford Museum; "There was never a time": quoted in Richard Hofstadter, *The Age of Reform* (New York: Random House, 1955), 109. 49

"A very decided drift": quoted in Samuel R. McKelvie, "What the Movies Mean to the Farmer," *Annals of the American Academy of Political and Social Sciences* 128 (November 1926): 132. 50 "Out of the freedom of his opportunities": quoted in Roderick Nash, *Wilderness and the American Mind* (New Haven: Yale University Press, 1967), 146; "Life of strenuous endeavor": ibid., 150. 51–52 "The times were boisterous": Donald Davidson, *The Tennessee* (New York: Rinehart and Co., 1948), 232–233. 52 "A selected place": John Coffee to Andrew Jackson, November 1, 1816, Alabama State Archives. 53 "It does not seem right": quoted in Louis A. Eckl, "Shoals Story is Recounted," *Florence* (Ala.) *Times*, special edition, October 1934, 9. 55 "The old order": *Florence* (Ala.) *Journal*, December 6, 1865, unpaginated; "The fact is": ibid., April 23, 1887, unpaginated; "75 Mile City": "Ford Plans a City 75 Miles in Length," *New York Times*, January 12, 1922, 1. 59 "The plight of the Negro farmer": R. R. Moton to Martin Madden, January 22, 1923, Henry Ford Museum. 60 "Would you": quoted in letter from W. G. Moore to E. G. Liebold, March 2, 1923, Henry Ford Museum. 62 "Ford felt": Liebold, oral history.

3 The Regionalists
63–64 "Kaleidoscopic," etc.: *Frank Lloyd Wright, An Autobiography* (New York: Duell, Sloan and Pearce, 1943), 253. 65 "Yankee expedients," etc.: Frank Lloyd Wright, *Experimenting with Human Lives* (Chicago: Ralph Fletcher Seymour, 1923), unpaginated. 67 "Your case": Wright, *Autobiography*, 294; "What looked like a lost cause": ibid., 291; "Immorality": ibid., 297. 69 "Prophetic at a crucial time": Frank Lloyd to Lewis Mumford, n.d. (c. 1957), Frank Lloyd Wright Archives; "If I could write like you": Frank Lloyd Wright to Lewis Mumford, January 24, 1931, Frank Lloyd Wright Archives. 70 "A technological genius": Lewis Mumford, *Sticks and Stones* (New York: Dover Publications, 1955), 102. 70 "A national program": Roy Lubove, *Community Planning in the 1920s: The Contribution of the Regional Planning Association of America* (Pittsburgh: University of Pittsburgh Press, 1963), 94. 71 "So long as men are forced": quoted in Giorgio Ciucci, *The American City* (Cambridge, Mass.: MIT Press, 1979), 293–387. 73–74 "The fourth migration": Lewis Mumford in *Survey Graphic* 7 (May 1925): 130–133. 75 "The greatest architect": quoted in Peter Eisenman, introduction to *Philip Johnson: Writings* (New York: Oxford University Press, 1979), 19. 76–77 "It was the turning point": Frederick Gutheim, "The Turning Point in Mr. Wright's Career," *AIA Journal* 69 (June 1980): 48–49; "This began to look": Wright, *Autobiography*, 364. 77 "Harmonize," etc.: Frank Lloyd Wright, *Modern Architecture: Being the Kahn Lectures for 1930* (Princeton, N.J.: Princton University Press, 1931), 78 "Is the city": ibid., 101; "The Machine," etc.: ibid., 108–109. 78–79 "Movies," etc.: ibid., 110; "Eventually we must live": ibid., 113. 79 "He is a man of common sense": quoted in Frederick Gutheim, ed., *Frank Lloyd Wright on Architecture* (New York: Grosset and Dunlap, 1951), 144. 80 "The best": Henry Ford, *Today and Tomorrow* (New York: Doubleday, Page and Company, 1926), 275; "To my mind": ibid., 250. 81 "The most valuable critic": Frank Lloyd Wright to Lewis Mumford, n.d. (c. June 1930), Frank Lloyd Wright Archives.

4 The Tennessee Valley Authority
83 "Regional self-consciousness": Paul K. Conklin, *The Southern Agrarians* (Knoxville: University of Tennessee Press, 1988), 32. 84 "Regionalism must be made": Lewis Mumford to Patrick Geddes, December 4, 1924, in Mumford, *Works and Days* (New York: Harcourt Brace Jovanovich, 1979), 107; "The reason regionalism was chosen": in Carl Sussman, ed., *Planning the Fourth Migration: The Neglected Vision of the Regional Planning Association of America* (Cambridge, Mass.: MIT Press, 1976), 28. 85 "He

told us": Louis Brownlow, *A Passion for Anonymity* (Chicago: University of Chicago Press, 1958), 270; "The pota-to-and-cabbage odor": Frederick Gutheim, "The Turning Point in Mr. Wright's Career," *AIA Journal* 69 (June 1980): 48–49. 86 "It was an enormous job," etc.: Frederick Gutheim, interview with author, Mitchellville, Md., December 30, 1991; "They were not sophisticated": ibid. 87 "Broadacre City": Frank Lloyd Wright, "Broadacre City: An Architect's Vision," *New York Times Magazine*, March 20, 1932, 8. 87–88 "I consented to join": Frank Lloyd Wright to Lewis Mumford, January 19, 1932 (Frank Lloyd Wright Archives). 90 "In enlarging the Muscle Shoals scheme": quoted in Walter L. Creese, *TVA s Public Planning* (Knoxville: University of Tennessee Press, 1991), 83; "TVA is the most profitable investment": quoted in Arthur M. Schlesinger, Jr., *The Politics of Upheaval* (Boston: Houghton Mifflin Company, 1960), 375. 91 "The largest electric facilities": "Thousand Hear Chieftain of Democracy Deliver Two Speeches in Shoals Cities," *The Florence* (Ala.) *Times*, January 21, 1933, 1; "I will put Muscle Shoals": "Other U.S. Watersheds May Benefit From Roosevelt's Visit to Shoals November 17," *Florence* (Ala.) *Times*, undated (c. November 1, 1934), 1. 92 "We are looking to a valley": from *The New York Times*, December 4, 1933,

quoted in Creese, *TVA's Public Planning*, 76; "A prophet's passion": Schlesinger, *Politics of Upheaval*, 365. 93 "Increasing danger": ibid., 366; "The RPAA": Gutheim, interview, December 30, 1991. 93–94 "An individual": From *The Washington Post*, February 18, 1934, quoted in Creese, *TVA's Public Planning*, 250–251. 94 "Wright was stimulated": Gutheim, interview, December 30, 1991.

5 At Taliesin
98 "There were doctors, painters": Olgivanna Wright, "The Last Days of Katherine Mansfield," *The Bookman*, March 1931, 6–13. 99 "The next America": quoted in Arthur M. Schlesinger, Jr., *The Politics of Upheaval* (Boston: Houghton Mifflin Company, 1960),152. 101 "I redrew rooms": Edgar Tafel, interview, New York, N.Y., November 27, 1991; "I have just finished": Nancy Willey to Frank Lloyd Wright, June 27, 1932, Frank Lloyd Wright Archives. 102 "Nothing is trivial": Frank Lloyd Wright to Nancy B. Willey, July 5, 1932, Frank Lloyd Wright Archives; "A wonderful world": Nancy B. Willey, video interview with Leif Anderson, March 12, 1989. 103 "Upside down house": *Minneapolis Star*, July 6, 1934, p. 12; "We'll try again": Frank Lloyd Wright to Nancy B. Willey, November 29, 1932, Frank Lloyd Wright Archives. 104 "I do not want": Nancy B. Willey to Frank Lloyd

Wright, November 26, 1933, Frank Lloyd Wright Archives; "Mr. Willey is thrilled": Nancy B. Willey to Frank Lloyd Wright, January 6, 1934, Frank Lloyd Wright Archives. 105 "We were so graciously received:" Nancy B. Willey, video interview with Leif Andersen; "Changes in the transportation system": Malcolm Willey, ed., *Recent Social Trends in the United States from the President s Research Committee on Social Trends* (New York: McGraw-Hill Book Company, 1933), 216. 106 "Lo!," and rest of anecdote: Nancy B. Willey, video interview with Leif Andersen; "Please remember": Nancy B. Willey to Frank Lloyd Wright, May 2, 1934, Frank Lloyd Wright Archives. 107 "Angled wide eaves": John Sergeant, *Frank Lloyd Wright's Usonian Houses* (New York: Watson-Guptill Publications, 1976), 23; "The horizontal joints": Eugene Masselink to Nancy B. Willey, June 6, 1934, Frank Lloyd Wright Archives. 108 "In which he predicts": Nancy B. Willey to Frank Lloyd Wright, n.d. (c. May 1, 1934), Frank Lloyd Wright Archives. 108–109 "Wayside restaurants," etc.: H. G. Wells, *Anticipations of the Reaction of Mechanical and Scientific Progress upon Human Life and Thought* (London: Chapman & Hall, Ltd., 1901), 57, 116–122.

6 Broadacre City
112 "Make me a half dozen": Edgar

Tafel, interview, New York, N.Y., November 27, 1991. 114 "Every Broadcare citizen": Frank Lloyd Wright, "Broadacre City: A New Community Plan," *Architectural Record* 77 (April 1935): 243–254. 114–115 "The houses of Broadacre City": Frank Lloyd Wright, "Broadacre City: Frank Lloyd Wright, Architect," *American Architect* 146 (May 1935): 55–62. 115 "The first...cross-section," etc.: Frank Lloyd Wright, "An Autobiography, Book Six: Broadacre City," offprint (A Taliesin Publication), 1943, 28. 116 "The ultimate importance": Norris Kelly Smith, *Frank Lloyd Wright: A Study in Architectural Content* (New York: Prentice-Hall, Inc., 1966), 170. 118 "Little farms": Wright, "Broadacre City," *Architectural Record*. 119 "The hope of Democracy": Frank Lloyd Wright, "Broadacres— A Dream of the City of the Future," reprint of radio address delivered at Rockefeller Center, May 9, 1935, *The Capital Times* (Madison, Wis.), June 5, 1935; "Despite his badly confused notion": Stephen Alexander, "Frank Lloyd Wright's Utopia," *New Masses*, June 18, 1935, 28. 120 "Now all this dreaming": Frank Lloyd Wright, letter in *New Masses*, July 23, 1935, 20. 121 "Just radical-minded enough": Baker Brownell to Frank Lloyd Wright, August 12, 1937, Frank Lloyd Wright Archives. 122 "Mr. Ford": Baker Brownell and Frank Lloyd Wright,

Architecture and Modern Life (New York: Harper and Brothers, 1937), 247. 124 "A wedge of concrete": ibid., 65; "Building more than a dam": ibid., 67. 125 "I don't want anybody coming in": quoted in Walter L. Creese, *TVA's Public Planning* (Knoxville: University of Tennessee Press, 1991), 253; "TVA is not attempting": ibid. 127 "Universal": Lewis Mumford, ed., *Roots of Contemporary American Architecture* (New York: Dover Publications, 1972), 29.

7 Houses and Housing
130 "More completely influenced": quoted in Edward Bok, *The Americanization of Edward Bok* (New York: Charles Scribner's Sons, 1921), 243. 130–131 "The several elements": "Organ of Integration," *Time*, April 11, 1932, 9. 132 "The small house problem," etc.: in Rudolph C. Henning, *At Taliesin* (Carbondale, Ill.: Southern Illinois University Press, 1991), 72–73. 135 "A four thousand dollar house": Eugene Masselink to Mrs. C. H. (Louise) Hoult, March 9, 1935, Frank Lloyd Wright Archives. 136 "A fresh projection," etc.: Eugene Masselink to Louise Hoult, August 16, 1935, Frank Lloyd Wright Archives. 137 "Were these...people": Robert D. Lusk to Frank Lloyd Wright, November 25, 1935, Frank Lloyd Wright Archives. 137–138 "The location": Robert D. Lusk to Frank Lloyd Wright, January

13, 1936, Frank Lloyd Wright Archives. 138 "Government loans": quoted in John Sergeant, *Frank Lloyd Wright's Usonian Houses* (New York: Watson-Guptill Publications, 1976), 30n. 141 "We hope to prove": "Highstown Resettlement Community Breaks Ground," *The New York Times*, August 6, 1935, 19. 142 "Had it not been for the idea": Quoted from an introduction to Clarence S. Stein, *Toward New Towns for America* in Howard Gillette, Jr., "Film as Artifact: The City (1939)," *American Studies* 18 (fall 1977): 72–85. 143 "In a day when": Laura Vitray, "Broadacres Offers New Ideal of Living," *Washington Post*, June 30, 1935, 5; "I have not invented": Karl Schriftgiesser, "Capital's Architecture Just Like Traffic," *Washington Post*, July 2, 1935, 12; "The finest city," etc.: Joseph L. Arnold, *The New Deal in the Suburbs* (Columbus, Ohio: Ohio State University Press, 1957), 85–86.

8 The Usonians
147 "The customers": Katherine Jacobs, interview with Abigail Malamed, Berkeley, Calif., March 7, 1992. 148 "What this country needs," etc.: ibid.; "I want to be able": Herbert Jacobs, *Building with Wright* (San Francisco: Chronicle Books, 1978), 10. ibid., 21–22. 150 "Gracious": "Usonian Architect," *Time*, January 17, 1938, 29–32; "Space": "Eight Houses for Modern Living," *Life*, September 26,

1938, 45–65. 152 "The best": Elizabeth B. Kassler, interview, December 28, 1991; "The purest example": John Sergeant, *Frank Lloyd Wright's Usonian Houses* (New York: Watson-Guptill Publications, 1976), 42. 154 "One of the most trenchant": Shelton Cheney, "Autobiography of Frank Lloyd Wright," *Saturday Review of Literature*, April 16, 1932, 16. 155 "I worked harder," etc.: Mildred B. Rosenbaum, interview, Florence, Ala., Janauary 2 and January 24, 1992. 156 Mildred B. Rosenbaum, interview, Florence, Ala., June 8, 1991. 157–158 Aaron G. Green to Frank Lloyd Wright, April 20, 1939, Domino's Center for Architecture and Design. 158 "My dear Green": Frank Lloyd Wright to Aaron G. Green, July 26, 1939, Domino's Center for Architecture and Design. 159 "A rather unusual circumstance": Aaron G. Green to Frank Lloyd Wright, August 2, 1939, Stanley Rosenbaum Papers; "In no attempt": Aaron G. Green to Frank Lloyd Wright, August 29, 1939, Stanley Rosenbaum Papers; "I intended": Frank Lloyd Wright to Aaron G. Green, September 15, 1939, Domino's Center for Architecture and Design. 160 "We itemize": Frank Lloyd Wright to Aaron G. Green, September 21, 1939, Domino's Center for Architecture and Design; "We are having": Aaron G. Green to Frank Lloyd Wright, October 21, 1939, Stanley Rosenbaum Papers; "Mr. Wright sug-

gests": Eugene Masselink to Aaron G. Green, October 25, 1939, Domino's Center for Architecture and Design; "The scope": Aaron G. Green to Frank Lloyd Wright, December 1, 1939, Stanley Rosenbaum Papers. 161 "Mr. R. Senior": Burt Goodrich to Frank Lloyd Wright, January 4, 1940, Frank Lloyd Wright Archives. 162–163 "When [Goodrich] went south": Edgar Tafel, *Years with Frank Lloyd Wright: Apprenticeship to Genius* (New York: Dover Publications, 1979), 191. 163 "Strange as it seems": Stanley Rosenbaum to Julian Altman, July 16, 1940, Stanley Rosenbaum Papers. 164–165 "The house is completed": Stanley Rosenbaum to Frank Lloyd Wright, August 23, 1940, Stanley Rosenbaum papers. 166 "Among present day architects": quoted in Barbara Branden, *The Passion of Ayn Rand* (New York: Doubleday & Company, 1986), 209. 168 "Why not": Geoffrey Baker, "At the Modern," *The New York Times*, November 24, 1940, K10, and response, ibid., December 15, 1940, K11; "Half modern": quoted in Peter Eisenman, introduction to *Philip Johnson: Writings* (New York: Oxford University Press, 1979).

9 World War II
171 Quoted in John Sergeant, *Frank Lloyd Wright's Usonian Houses* (New York: Watson-Guptill Publications, 1976), 201. 172–173 "My dear

Madame President": Frank Lloyd Wright to Eleanor Roosevelt, July 12, 1935, Frank Lloyd Wright Archives. 174–175 "Deplored the violence": Frank Lloyd Wright, "Good Morning Mr. Evjue," *A Taliesin Square-Paper*, no. 3, June 1941, 1. 175 "Why don't you contribute," etc.: quoted in Donald Leslie Johnson, *Frank Lloyd Wright versus America: The 1930s* (Cambridge, Mass.: MIT Press, 1990), 325, 328. 176 "You know," etc.: quoted in Brendan Gill, *Many Masks: A Life of Frank Lloyd Wright* (New York: G. P. Putman's Sons, 1987, 417: "A notorious name-dropper": Bruce Brooks Pfeiffer, interview, March 11, 1992. 178 "This is to you," etc.: Frank Lloyd Wright to Henry A. Wallace, January 22, 1943, and Henry A. Wallace to Frank Lloyd Wright, March 3, 1943, Frank Lloyd Wright Archives; "A few [Hollywood directors]": Frank Lloyd Wright to Marc Connelly, March 17, 1943, Frank Lloyd Wright Archives; "I do not know": Frank Lloyd Wright to Frederic Delano, March 5, 1943, Frank Lloyd Wright Archives. 180 "Although there were": Allan D. Wallis, *Wheel Estate* (New York: Oxford University Press, 1991), 222. 183 "Where the details": Marshall Erdman, interview, April 15, 1992; "Upper middle third," etc.: Frank Lloyd Wright, *The Natural House* (New York: Bramhall House, 1954), 197–202. 185 "Modifications": Rick Beard, Priscilla Henken, and David

Henken, *Realizations of Usonia: Frank Lloyd Wright in Westchester* (Yonkers: The Hudson River Museum, 1985), 15. 186 "Been stimulated," etc.: Mary S. Palmer to Frank Lloyd Wright, April 17, 1950, Frank Lloyd Wright Archives; "Their advice was simple": Mary S. Palmer, interview, Ann Arbor, Michigan, March 27, 1992.

10 Today and Tomorrow
189 "The indulged children": William Strauss and Neil Howe, *Generations*

(New York: William Morrow and Company, 1991), 241. 190 "Creative rather than possessive impulses": quoted in Lewis Mumford, *The Story of Utopias* (New York: Viking Press, 1965), 87; "Embodiment of human freedom": Frank Lloyd Wright, *The Living City* (New York: New American Library, 1958), 110. 191 "Is already so well organized": ibid., 181; "Architecture and acreage": ibid., 123. 195 "Not as an add-on": "The Art of Design Management," in *Design for America's*

Third Century, ed. Walter Hoving (New York: Tiffany and Co., 1975), 102.

11 Epilogue
202 "The law of adaptation": "Form and Function," in *Roots of Contemporary Architecture*, ed. Lewis Mumford (New York: Reinhold Publishing Co., 1952).

PHOTOGRAPHY CREDITS

INDEX

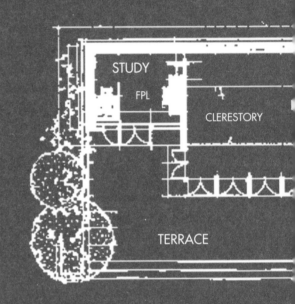

USONIAN HOUSE FOR

MILDRED & STANLEY ROSENBAUM
FLORENCE, ALABAMA

FRANK LLOYD WRIGHT ARCHITECT
1940 ■ 1948